Retreading My Life

By
Richard O'Connell

MAPLE
PUBLISHERS

Retreading My Life

Author: Richard O'Connell

Copyright © 2026 Richard O'Connell

The author asserts the moral right to be identified as the author of this work.

The right of Richard O'Connell to be identified as author of this work has been asserted by the author in accordance with section 77 and 78 of the Copyright, Designs and Patents Act 1988.

First Published in 2026

ISBN 978-1-83538-773-3 (Paperback)
      978-1-83538-784-9 (Hardback)
      978-1-83538-774-0 (E-Book)

Cover Design and Book Layout by:
    Maple Publishers
    www.maplepublishers.com

Published by:
    Maple Publishers
    Fairbourne Drive, Atterbury,
    Milton Keynes,
    MK10 9RG, UK
    www.maplepublishers.com

The views expressed in this work are solely those of the author and do not reflect the opinions of Publishers, and the Publisher hereby disclaims any responsibility for them. This book should not be used as a substitute for the advice of a competent authority, admitted or authorized to advise on the subjects covered.

A CIP catalogue record for this title is available from the British Library.

All rights reserved. No part of this book may be reproduced or translated by any form or by any means, electronic or mechanical, including photocopying, recording or by any information storage and retrieval system without written permission from the author.

Contents

Chapter 1 – Intro 5
Chapter 2 – Setting out on life 16
Chapter 3 – Education and Employment 29
Chapter 4 – Exmouth 44
Chapter 5 – Starting Bandvulc 54
Chapter 6 – Married Life 73
Chapter 7 – Flying 82
Chapter 8 – Scotland 91
Chapter 9 – Big Business 95
Chapter 10 – And in Conclusion 117

This book is dedicated to my wife Shela, our children Ryan and Samantha (Sam), who have given me constant love, friendship and support along my journey.

Chapter 1

Intro

Our lives roll out as an ever-changing tapestry. Some lives develop in pedigree lines such as royal families, aristocracy and secular religions. Others develop in somewhat more haphazard ways, and I fell into the latter category.

I was born on Monday, 17th October 1949 in Broomborough Hospital, Totnes, Devon. It was a day when Herbert Morrison, the Labour government's campaign manager warned the country that 'You will soon hear the government's decision on measures to bring Britain's economy into balance'. So as far as governing of the country by any party, nothing much has changed in my 70-plus years.

Broomborough had been a workhouse in previous years and was described as 'having the capacity to accommodate 380 paupers', but in 1948 became an NHS maternity unit. The town of Totnes lies at the end of the tidal reach of the River Dart. The river carries a rather sinister quotation which sadly seems to hold true 'Dart, Dart, cruel Dart, every year thou claim'st a heart'.

My parents were a couple who seemed to have arrived at marriage more by convenience than love although they stuck together for their entire lives and never strayed.

My father, John O'Connell (alias Jack), was born in Limerick on 24th June 1900. The family lived in a small two-bedroom house near Caherconlish, grandly called Castle Irkin. There was no running water, just an outside trough with a pump and an outside chemical toilet. The house was heated by the standard Irish open peat fired stove. In 1911 the family consisted of Jack Senior (my grandfather, aged 47), Eliza Sweeny (my grandmother, aged 46) together with their children James aged 17, Eliza aged 11 and Jack recorded as aged nine. Jack's birth certificate shows, however, that he was born in 1900 and so some of

My Irish Grandmother

the records are distinctly somewhat 'Irish'. The census also shows that Eliza had five other children who had died in infancy. Neither of the parents could read or write. Also living in the house at the time were Patrick Sweeney, aged 38 (brother-in-law), and Bridget Sweeney, aged 79 (mother-in-law).

Jack O'Connell Senior died in 1923 aged 59, apparently from blood poisoning.

Eliza Senior died on the 9th December 1954, aged 89 years.

People in the house slept where they lay and used candles and oil lamps for lighting. They all lived through 'The War of Independence' and had experienced the wrath of consumption plus the Black and Tans with their retribution upon the Irish population for their actions to wrest independence from the British. Jack and his siblings were educated in a classroom and learnt the three Rs and did not go to Hedge School like many of the less fortunate. When he left school, he started his own business with a horse and cart drawing stone from a quarry near Caherconlish into Limerick. Work started to dry up when the quarry bought a traction engine. Despite the horse hauliers protesting and picketing the quarry, as usual technology won the day and the days of domestic road haulage by horse went into decline. Most horses were also being bought up to supply the war in Europe. With a lack of work, and the worsening political situation and Jack wishing to stay attached to his kneecaps, he went to look for a better life in England. In 1920, at the age of 20, he arrived in England with a suitcase and 2/6d in his pocket. He bought a packet of Woodbines and sat on the dock while he worked out his options.

The work options for Irish immigrants with little education were limited in 1920, as was finding accommodation, with several boarding houses displaying signs stating, 'No Blacks or Irish'.

Jack somehow managed to acquire a labouring job with The Sheffield Construction Company who specialised in major industrial projects. That saw him settled for a few years until the depression struck in 1930 and he found himself unemployed.

He walked the streets and lanes of Sheffield looking for work and was fortunate to happen upon a farm which also had a butchery business. The farmer's name was Wragg, and he gave Jack a job. He lived and worked on the farm for about two years until the recession began to ease and the Sheffield Construction Company once again began hiring. Jack returned to the Sheffield Construction Company and moved with them to a construction site in Paignton, Devon. This site was at Holcombe where a new gasometer was being installed. The workers lived in rented accommodation near the site, but I never learnt much about this.

When the work at this site was completed, they moved to a construction site at Staverton near Totnes in Devon. This was quite an ambitious project for the time and consisted of building a leat from the River Dart, to supply a new hydro-electric plant. The project was made even more challenging by the occasional unexpected flooding of the site and by the river breaking its banks during periods of high rainfall. This resulted in the wooden forms for casting the concrete occasionally being washed down river and teams of men sent to retrieve them. It seems that the workers camped out on the site here for a lot of the time during the construction. There were many Irish among them which led to them being quite a boisterous group. It was during Jack's time working here that his eyes fell upon Ethel Napper.

Ethel Napper was the daughter of Charles and Ellen Napper. She was born in Burlescombe, Somerset on 16th February 1911. Charles Napper, Ethel's father, was born at Ide near Exeter on 14th May 1877. When leaving school, he started out as a labourer but applied to join the Marines and was enlisted at Taunton on 14th November 1895 aged 18. His enlistment describes him as 5'6" tall with black hair, blue eyes and a fair complexion. When he was discharged in 1901, he worked on the railways.

Ethel's mother, Ellen, was born 'Ellen Jane Jeanes' and baptised in the Parish of Stoke St Gregory, Somerset on 27th June 1880. Although never previously married, when Ellen was married to Charles Napper on 21st March 1903, her surname had changed to Squire with her father named as Richard Squire. This has never been resolved.

Ellen, aged 23, and Charles, aged 25, were married at the Bridgewater registry office on 21st March 1903. They lived in a railway house beside the main line at Burlescombe. Sadly, Charles died of a heart attack on 26th April 1917 aged 41, leaving Ellen with five young children.

Following the death of Charles, the railway authorities took pity on the family and moved them to a cottage in Staverton beside the Totnes to Buckfastleigh branch line. Ellen's job was to operate the level crossing gates for which she was given a small income. This would seem rather extravagant now, as there was only one other property located on the other side of the railway line, namely the hydro-electric plant.

Although it was called a house, it was not truly a house. The area had been subjected to regular flooding, and over the years it was only the top floor of the house that was lived in, reached by a flight of steps leading from the road. The door led into a kitchen/dining area with a large black Lidstone stove as the only source of heating and cooking. Two doors led away from this room, one to a galley type kitchen with a small bedroom alongside it and the other door led to a sitting room and farther bedroom. On the wall in the living room was some sort of device that warned when a train was approaching. Stacked next to the device were a pile of metal objects about four inches in diameter and about half an inch thick. These were what were called detonators, and three were to be placed on the railway line to stop the train in case of an emergency. They were very highly explosive, but I was allowed to play with them when visiting if nothing else was to hand. Water was supplied by a hand pump from the leat. Around the back of the house via the vegetable garden stood a small outhouse built against the house wall which housed the chemical toilet complete with a selection of torn newspaper sheets on a wire hook. Between the house and level crossing there was a small fenced off area where Ellen kept chickens. Ellen was a strict Christian and the children all regularly attended Sunday school and church. My Mum, Ethel, up until her death, always knelt by her bed and said a prayer before retiring for the night.

The children were Beatrice (eldest), Leonard, Ethel (my mother), Clifford and Blanche (youngest). Clifford was a somewhat backward member of the family and lived at home with Ellen until almost the end of his life. He was quite capable of holding down a job and worked on the Dartington Hall estate for most of his life. He tended Ellen's garden and looked after the chickens. He was also in charge of the chemical toilet which was used to fertilise the garden.

The children attended the school in the village and there was also a Girl Guide group that Ethel joined, and they put on shadow plays in the village hall. The family were confined to the village with an occasional ride into Totnes on the train using the travel vouchers that were supplied to employees of GWR.

Leonard became a porter at Staverton railway station and progressed to becoming a signalman.

My mother, Ethel Napper, had little recollection of her father. She was six years old when, after the burial of her father, the family moved to Staverton.

As the children grew into their teens they left school and had to look for employment. Beatrice went into service, but I do not know where. My mother went into service at the Staverton vicarage where the vicar was the Reverend Edward Drake-Brockman (he was the vicar from 1922–1957). She became well known for her cake-making skills with the vicar apparently remarking that 'Ethel puts a wonderful top hat on her cakes'. She had a reputation for being somewhat feisty although she, nor my father, never laid a hand on my brother John or myself. She always liked the outdoor life and used to catch eels in the leat using a stocking filled with chicken entrails. The eels would hang onto the stocking when it was placed in the water, and she would quickly pull them out while they were still gripping the stocking. On occasional Sunday mornings she would bunk off going to church and take herself on walks through the woods beside the River Dart. Late in her teens she met a man whom she mentioned from time to time and whom she had seemed very fond of. He had a motorbike and would bring her cakes that he had baked himself which was quite unusual for a man in those times. She was heartbroken, though, when he crashed his motorbike and was killed coming to visit her. My father Jack, then began to attract her attention although she said that she was initially frightened of him, being 11 years older than her. She was also shocked

Mum and Dad on their wedding day 1937

when he kissed her on their first date, but love seemed to have endured. There was a fear among young women at that time of 'being left on the shelf' and becoming an 'Old Maid' living all alone. This fear had been brought about in recent years, because of the shortage of eligible bachelors after the First World War where so many had been killed or critically injured. There was also another complication in their relationship; Ethel was Church of England and Jack was Roman Catholic. When being noticed in the Staverton Parish that they were a couple, some anonymous letters started to be sent to Ethel discrediting Jack. Jack went to discuss this with the vicar, and the letters stopped.

In 1937, Ethel and Jack were married in Totnes and rented a flat at Number 1 Redworth Court, which is close to Totnes railway station. Jack left the construction company and started working for Dartington Hall, which was a large estate owned by the Elmhirst family. The estate consisted of farms, sawmills, and a private school. For their honeymoon, they went to Jersey which was quite an adventure for my mother who had never been much farther than Totnes.

Not long after moving into the flat they moved again to number 7 Broom Park, a house on a housing estate owned by Dartington Hall in Dartington. My brother John was born on 19th June 1940 while they lived at that address. War had broken and an air raid shelter was built down the lane from Broom Park towards the hamlet of Week. During an air raid alert, they had to leave their house and walk the quarter mile to the shelter. Jack, was exempted from military service and became part of the war effort via a different avenue. He was put in a reserved occupation to produce charcoal which was in high demand for gas masks and explosives. This took him away from home, working in woodland around Morton Hampstead and East Anstey. He became fascinated by the antics of the woodland ants which he often mentioned during his lifetime, leading to a rather comical experience in the latter stage of his life when he was suffering from a confused mind; but more of that later.

As the war progressed movement around the Dartington area became more and more restricted. American troops poured into the area and were hidden in the woods and lanes. Many took part in the

Dads horses in Totnes 1940's

disastrous Operation Tiger, a mock D-Day landing at Slapton where around one thousand American servicemen lost their lives. A large pond was built behind the School at Dartington where the amphibious tanks were tested to ensure they were watertight. All persons travelling within the restricted area had to carry a pass. Then on the morning of 6th June 1944 the local inhabitants awoke to a scene of deserted roads and woods, the D-Day invasion had begun and free movement returned.

After the war the movie makers moved into the area making a film called Escape starring Rex Harrison, Peggy Cummins and William Hartnell. The story centred around an escaped Dartmoor prisoner who was hiding out in the area. Staverton railway station, Staverton church and Nappers Crossing are featured in the story. My mother remembers Rex Harrison dropping his script into the leat and turning the air 'blue' with his language. The movie was released in 1948. My gran's house is clearly visible in the background of the Nappers crossing scene.

During the war years there was a big demand for horses. The shortage of petrol meant that farms were reliant on horsepower plus the coal mines and delivery companies. Jack saw an opportunity to make some money from his Irish expertise in horses and using his contacts that he had made on Dartmoor during his charcoal burning, plus his contacts in Ireland. He started a trade in horse dealing. He rented several fields around Totnes, particularly where the by-pass is now situated plus some buildings at Week village just outside of Dartington. He ran this business whilst still working for Dartington Hall.

He also managed to buy a bungalow in Paignton, mainly by accident. Whilst constructing some fencing around a new housing estate near Kings Ash he got talking to the estate agent. The agent asked him if he would like to buy one of the bungalows. Jack said he did not have that type of money, but the agent persisted, saying that if he could give a small deposit he could arrange for a tenant, and the rent would pay the mortgage. This was arranged and a tenant family called Ring moved in.

Jack was now starting to move up the business ladder but as is often the case something comes along to thwart your plans and Jack's growing success had not gone unnoticed. He was called in by the management of Dartington Hall around 1948 and told that although self-employed, he would need to make a choice. He could not run his own business and work for Dartington Hall. This caused Jack somewhat of a quandary. He decided that he would probably have enough money to put down a deposit on a small farm and be master of his own destiny. Having looked at a few places it fell between one at Slapton and one at Ashford, a small hamlet near Aveton Gifford. He decided on Helliers Farm at Ashford, a farm of 21 acres with a farmhouse and buildings dating back to 1749. In view of the condition of the buildings it didn't look like much had been done to it since then. The house and buildings stood high on the side of a valley and were south-facing which meant they enjoyed good sunlight. It was a traditional four walls type of building with four bedrooms, a kitchen, two reception rooms and a cold room for perishable goods. The house had no electricity, gas or mains water supply and its sole cooking facility was an old black Lidstone stove. The water was supplied by a spring high up on the hill which was fed into a stone tank about 4'x6'x3' high. Although the water source came from high on the hill, the whole time we lived there it never dried up. We had the occasional worm or slug appear out of the tap, though. The pipework from the reservoir was made of steel which ran underground across several fields. and over the years suffered from severe corrosion. We had to repair the occasional leak by digging down and then wrapping a length of car tyre inner tube around the pipe and securing with wire. The farm was approached by a lane which had two connections to the main road. The farm buildings lay on the higher side of the lane dug into the hillside. This area was referred to as 'The Quarry' as this is what it resembled. There was a cowshed which could house about eight cows at a time for milking with a hay barn on the second floor. The building was built of Devon granite stone. Across the yard were a couple of traditional low level stone pig houses with earth floors. One slightly larger stock shed stood beside these. In the centre of the yard sat the manure heap.

Chapter 2

Setting out on life

I was nine months old when the family left Dartington and moved into the farm. According to my brother, who was nine at the time, the move was somewhat chaotic. A memorable moment seems to have been transporting an exceptionally large Welsh linen cupboard on top of an Austin 7 which started to lift the roof off. When it was unloaded at the farm it wouldn't fit through the door and so Jack sawed it in half and then nailed it back together again. The house was a far cry from what my mother had been used to. There was no electricity or mains sanitation. Heating was by open fires and cooking by a solitary Lidstone stove. Lighting was supplied by candles and two Tilley lamps. During the initial moving in period, some modernisation occurred in the form of a Rayburn cooker to replace the Lidstone, plus a hot water supply from a back boiler. The hot water tank was located in a bedroom above the kitchen. Although the Rayburn kept the kitchen warm by day it did not have the capacity to run through the night and had to be cleaned and relit each morning. That meant that during very cold winter nights we were freezing, and the cold-water supply frequently froze solid. A trick to try to prevent this was to leave the kitchen tap slowly running when we went to bed but this usually resulted in a large icicle hanging from the tap in the morning and still no water.

Being a baby when we moved, I remember nothing of the early years at the farm and rely very much on accounts from my brother John. He developed a cough during the move and a spot was found on his lung which indicated TB. He had to rest in bed with plenty of fresh air for several weeks, which for a nine-year-old child was quite challenging. Antibiotics were still very much restricted at that time but fortunately he made a full recovery. I apparently also became ill with gastroenteritis and was also quite poorly at about the same time.

On the farm circa 1952

Jack had about half a dozen milking cows in Dartington and was already supplying milk via churns to Dawes Creamery which was based in Totnes. When moving into the Helliers he had to build a platform out of railway sleepers in the hedge on the main road so that the milk lorry could collect the full churns and leave us some empty ones. A label would be tied to each churn with the name and farm address. At the end of each month the milk cheque would arrive. At the creamery, the churns were loaded onto a conveyor and a man would lift each churn lid and sniff the milk to ensure that it had not gone sour or been contaminated. Sour milk on hot summer nights was always a problem and so we cooled it with an apparatus that used water from the spring to run through cooling pipes put into the churns. Another problem with the milk could be, if one of the cows ate wild garlic and it was not spotted in time before it went into the churn. Not long after establishing the small herd it was struck by some sort of virus whereby the cows aborted their calves. This was devastating as the milk supply which we all relied upon began to run down and a very lean time ensued while we worked through this virus.

I remember nothing really until I was about two and a half years old. I was always very adventurous, and a series of barricades were constructed around the house to stop me escaping. These were mainly made of old bedsteads. My parents spent little time with me during the day and I had no other children to play with. Dad was always up at 5 am to milk the cows and Mum would be busy getting the food ready for the day plus washing and ironing. We had no electricity and therefore no refrigerator or washing machine, kettle, etc. We had a room at the back of the house that we called the dairy for storing perishable food. It was half buried and had a cold stone floor and even in summer always kept cool. The nearest village was Aveton Gifford which was a mile away. Mum never learnt to drive and so would sometimes cycle there or take the bus if Dad was away and she needed something urgently. When I was about three years old it became impossible to keep me in and I spent my time wandering the fields with our two dogs, Pat and Bob. Pat was a Cairn terrier and Bob was a Shetland sheepdog cross collie. Pat was an incredibly good hunting dog and would tackle mice, rats and rabbits without fear. He would crash through brambles and down rabbit holes looking for his prey. Bob was more cautious and more intelligent. He would watch Pat while lying away in the field and when Pat's commotion would cause a rabbit to flee Bob would have him. Bob was my escort. I would hold his collar and he would patiently allow me to totter along with him while Pat ran on ahead. When Bob caught a rabbit, he would bring it back and drop it at my feet. I would swing it over my shoulder and totter back home with it. If Pat caught a rabbit, it belonged to Pat and no matter how much I shouted or pulled at it, Pat would not give up his prize, and so Bob and I would follow him back home where Mum would wrestle it from him. In the early 1950s rabbits were a big problem. Crops were blighted from them and in particular anything growing within twenty feet of a hedge. Farmers tried everything to keep them at bay, but nothing worked long term.

In 1953 a disease called myxomatosis arrived in the UK from France. It was a fatal disease for rabbits spread by fleas. It was a horrible disease which led to a slow lingering death and rabbits could be seen by roadsides and hedges covered in sores and barely alive. The dogs knew there was something wrong and would not go near them. It did, however, bring a respite to farmers who would now be able to expect reasonable harvests. This brought to an end my hunting trips.

Life on the farm was rather solitary as a toddler, but that was the only life I knew. When the sun went down it got dark, and when it came up it got light. It was possible to cheat the dark with candles and one of our two Tilley lamps. Voices occasionally came out of a box called a wireless which was on a table near the front room window. Summers were beautiful with flowers and birds singing, but winters were long, dark and cold. On very cold winter nights Mum would put me to bed and place my Dad's old Home Guard coat over me for extra warmth. It was, though, a magical time of life. There was Christmas, when presents were delivered by Father Christmas into an old pillowcase hung in the front room. There were tooth fairies, old barns that were empty because ghosts lived in them, and the sinister elm tree about half a mile away in the lane where a local man had hung himself, being discovered in the morning by the postman. There was also an old lady who sat on a log at the end of our lane from time to time feeding the birds. She was always dressed in black and wore a round black crinkly hat. She was a very gentle soul and lived on a farm about a mile away. During my time alone I apparently decided I needed some friends and so my little brain conjured up three imaginary characters. They all had names, but how I arrived at them I don't know. There were Cocacombes, Lugs and Linklees. Cocacombes was always good and helpful, Lugs was always bad and Linklees was unpredictable. My world was beginning to develop. My relationship with my Dad was rather distant as he worked seven days a week and 365 days a year. There was one break in this routine when every other Sunday we would all travel to Staverton to visit our nan at the railway crossing and have lunch there. On the return journey Dad would sometimes fall asleep and bounce off the hedge which together with Mum shouting at him would revive him. The cars that we used had all seen better days and were always filled with eye watering fumes from the engine and exhaust which meant a period of rehabilitation after returning home. They also had no heaters at that time, and so Mum would sit the dogs on her feet in the front to keep warm. Our nan was a very thrifty person and could make a meal out of virtually nothing. One of her sons, Clifford, lived with her. Although he had a job working at the Dartington Hall estate, he was incapable of looking after himself and lived with her until later in life when he went a little crazy and was sectioned and put in Digby mental hospital in Exeter. When our nan died quite a large sum of money was found hidden in the property. It caused a bit of a problem as the notes were well out of date, but the bank did eventually change them.

Across the valley from our farm was Manor Garage. In the winter it lay frost-ridden for most of the day on account of being in the bottom of the dip and facing north. The owners were Mr and Mrs Ellis and they had a daughter called Bridget. Mrs Ellis was a kindly soul and had sadly lost a son called Jeremy from cancer in 1954. Jeremy was the same age as my brother John. Morris Edgcumbe, who worked at the garage, would bring our daily papers from the village shop and place them in the gate at the bottom of a field in front of our house. We had trained Bob the dog to fetch the papers. Each day we would say 'Papers' to him, and he would dutifully run down the field, pull the papers out of the gate and bring them into the kitchen. One hot day he returned empty handed, or should I say empty mouthed. He crept under the kitchen table looking very sheepish. We kept asking him where the papers were but he just lay under the table looking sad. We retraced his route to the gate but could find no papers. On the way back up the hill we walked across to a cow watering trough and discovered the papers floating in the water. He had stopped for a drink but forgot he was holding the papers.

Another incident that involved Bob was the mysterious disappearing tortoise called Joey. My brother had a tortoise, and every now and then he would be discovered on the main road about half a mile away. The mystery was solved one day when Bob was discovered with Joey in his mouth heading for the highway.

There is a nine-year difference between John my brother and myself, John being older. John was very much an academic but on weekends and holidays he would have to get to work with Dad, ably assisted by myself. Hoeing turnips was one of the worst jobs. Hours on end slowly walking in silence with a hoe picking out a gap for a solitary turnip to survive. Another unpopular task was moving the electric fence to provide another six feet strip of kale for the cows to eat. On a muddy steep field in the cold winter rain it was not an easy task. Having moved it, it was then necessary to check that it wasn't shorting out on any leaves. Walking the length of the fence when it was live and trying to pick off a leaf without getting a shock was quite a challenge. The hay harvest, however, could be a very pleasant time of year if the weather held out. A contractor would cut the hay and we would turn it to dry with a various range of contraptions. We grew about five acres of hay, always from the same field but it gave a good yield. Our farm was quite steep and Jack used to make what he called a 'slide'. It was usually a couple of telegraph poles in parallel and cross braced with other pieces of timber. In the early days we used horsepower to drag it but then moved on to a small Bristol 20 caterpillar tractor.

I started school at Aveton Gifford in September 1954 aged four. We had to take a gym bag with us complete with gym shoes, shorts and tee shirt. Mum made me a gym bag out of a pink pillowcase and sewed a drawstring into the opening. Why she chose a pink pillowcase, I don't

Potato harvest with my dad brother and uncle

know. I was introduced to Miss Farmer who was going to be my teacher. I guess she was around 30 years old and a very kindly person. My first morning in the classroom was absolute torture I had never been with a group of children before and I found the noise unbearable. So much so that I made several visits to the toilet for some quiet. The classroom was heated by a big cylindrical cast iron stove which had a bucket of coke alongside it. Miss Farmer would occasionally grab the bucket and shake a quantity of coke in through a small top opening. The fires were lit before we got to school by Miss Putt who was the school caretaker. On cold mornings we would warm our third-of-a-pint of milk that we were given each day beside the stove. The toilets were in an unheated adjoining outbuilding where we washed our hands with carbolic soap in cold water.

At lunchtime we would form lines and walk out through the school gate and across the road to the village hall. The meals were delivered to the hall in large aluminium canisters and reheated in the kitchen there by the dinner ladies. Mrs Elliot seemed to be head dinner lady and was not to be crossed. You had to eat all your lunch. If you wanted to leave any, you had to take your plate up to the teachers' table where three teachers passed judgment on your plate. Grisly meat was judged to be acceptable to leave but greens had to be eaten. After lunch we would trek back to the school and enjoy a certain amount of playtime. The school had two playgrounds, one for the infant class and a larger one for the older pupils. We had to stay outside in the playground no matter what the weather until the bell rang to start lessons. On cold wet days with only shorts, socks and sandals, plus a coat, playtimes were not always a pleasant affair. Adjoined to the infants' playground was a field that was higher up and accessed by some concrete steps. The field, which for some strange reason was called 'Pullies', was about a quarter of an acre. It was where the sports events were held. Sometimes on a warm summer's day we would be led up there during lesson time and read a story. The field was next to Saunders butchers which had its own abattoir and so we were often treated to the sounds and smells and noises that went with it. The school bought a Suffolk Punch mower to cut the grass and we were allowed to use it by ourselves in break times. School health and safety has moved on a little since then, I gather.

I enjoyed the sports days; lying around in the fresh cut grass on a hot summer's day seemed to make everything OK with the world. We were also introduced to swimming by being driven to a school in Kingsbridge that had a swimming pool (unheated, of course). It was here that I gained my 25-yard swimming certificate. The first certificate I had ever been awarded.

Many children came from farming backgrounds, and it seemed that there were always a few children covered in patches of iodine to treat their ringworm. Mumps, measles, chickenpox, and whooping cough all swept through the school from time to time, but we all seemed to pull through. We also suffered from chilblains in winter, an ailment that is not seen today. The middle school class was taught by Mrs Townsend who lived in Yealmpton and rode in every day on the Western National bus that travelled from Plymouth to Dartmouth. She had her special seat reserved at the back next to where the conductor stood. When you reached Mrs Townsend's class life began to get serious; she was not to be crossed. Although extremely strict she was caring in her own way. On 26th January 1943, seven Focke Wulf fighter bombers bombed and strafed the village of Aveton Gifford around 4 o'clock in the afternoon. Mrs Townsend was out with a group of children at the time and she pushed them into the hedge and lay on top of them for protection.

When I was six years old, I had been suffering for some time with sudden stomach cramps and was diagnosed with appendicitis. I was admitted to Kingsbridge hospital in February 1956. Mum was terribly ill with the flu at the time and so John, my brother, took me to the hospital on the bus. I remember that it was very cold with a lot of snow around. Being left on my own in a hospital ward was very scary. I was prepared for the operation and given an enema which was a rather strange experience for a six-year-old who had never been aware of any medical procedures. The operation was performed using ether. I can still remember a big rubber mask being put over my face and told to breathe. When I awoke, I felt extremely sick and was desperate for a drink of water. The nurse said that I should not drink, as it would make me sick. I remember pleading for a sip of water which she gave me and sure enough I was sick. There were two other children on the ward at the time who had had their tonsils removed going through the same experience. Once I began to recover, hospital life wasn't so bad. It was warm and the food was good. The hospital had its own garden complete with gardener. I had a huge thick sticking plaster around my waist and was kept on the ward for about two weeks until they were sure that I had completely healed. Removing the sticking plaster was the next traumatic event. Being laid on my back and then having it unceremoniously whipped off. The irony of the whole episode was, that they discovered there was nothing wrong with my appendix.

I returned to school but within the next two years another medical event arose. Sometimes I would feel quite faint for no apparent reason. Particularly after a long journey in Dad's fume filled car. I was sent to see a specialist at Kingsbridge hospital who diagnosed an overactive thyroid, and I was put on a course of phenobarbitone to slow me down. There was talk of removing part of my thyroid which thankfully never took place. Eventually I was referred to another consultant who said that there was nothing wrong with me and I was just a kid who ran around too much.

These were times of austerity following the war and when Great Britain was quite regimented. At the end of a cinema film or theatre play we would stand in silence for God save the queen. Shops closed on Wednesday afternoons for what was known as 'early closing day' to counteract opening on Saturday mornings. They were closed all day on Sundays. If you owned a shotgun, you just went to the post office and bought a licence for ten shillings. In 1956, the BBC was allowed to broadcast television on weekdays between 9 am and 11 pm, with no more than two hours before 1 pm. There was also a period between 6 pm and 7 pm when no television was broadcast. This period was used by parents to trick young children into thinking that the evening's television had finished so they would go to bed without complaint – it was known as the 'toddlers' truce'.!!! We also always addressed an adult as Mister or Missus or Miss followed by their surname, never by their Christian name. It seemed to be a time when nearly everyone smoked. Offices, theatres and cinemas would be in a constant haze of tobacco smoke. Capital punishment was still in use and I can remember some solemn mornings at primary school when we were told that a criminal was being hanged that day.

I progressed through primary school and became quite accomplished at reading and enjoyed nature and geography. Maths was not my strong point though, and something I would struggle with throughout my academic career. I did manage to scrape through the 11-plus exam which meant I would follow in my brother's footsteps to Kingsbridge Grammar school. I never realised the relative freedom that we enjoyed at primary school until I started at Kingsbridge Grammar. I was now once again, a small fish in a big pond and that pond held quite a few sharks.

Your uniform was all important, and I remember it was the first time that I had worn long trousers. They were grey serge and irritated my legs; Mum not being able to afford flannel ones. I was issued with a bus pass and caught the twenty-past-eight morning bus from outside the entrance to Manor Garage which was the garage on the other side of the valley owned by the Ellis family.

The bus journey took 25 minutes and dropped us off at the Kingsbridge bus station which was situated by the railway station and later moved to Kingsbridge quay when the railway station closed. There was then a ten-minute walk up the hill to school. The school seemed intimidatingly large compared to the primary school I had been used to although the complete roll call was only about 300 students. It was separated into boys and girls, with separate playgrounds, but we could see the girls through the wire fencing. Each morning when we arrived we had to form lines in the playground according to our class number. This was done no matter what the weather and we were watched over by the prefects. If you were caught talking or missing your cap you would be issued with a detention. We then trailed into the assembly hall leaving our coats, hats and bags in the cloakroom on the way. Having assembled in our respective rows with the junior classes at the front leading up to seniors at the back, the teachers would appear on stage. There would then be a loud bang which came from the door to the side of the stage and signalled that the headmaster was making his entrance. His name was Fred Lisle. There would then be hymns and prayers after which we would file out and attend the first lesson of the day. There would of course be a farting competition during the silent parts of the assembly but one had to be careful not to be caught giggling by one of the prefects who oversaw the event from a gallery.

Kingsbridge Grammar school was very academic with only woodwork as a hands-on practical subject for boys. We were taught Latin and French and I soon discovered that I had no aptitude in speaking a foreign language especially Latin. When in my lifetime would I need to say 'The spears of the Romans are in the boats of the Gauls' in Latin? French was also a subject that I could see no need for, never having travelled farther than Exeter. I did, however, enjoy physics and this was the only O level that I gained at school. Many changes took place during my time at the school. The boys and girls became integrated, plus the school became a Comprehensive. The sudden introduction of girls into a class of 14-year-old boys resulted in some strange behaviour which is probably better not mentioned here! We were also introduced to the noble art of rugby. We had only just got used to football for which none of us had great enthusiasm, including the teacher. Rugby was a whole new experience and the Secondary Modern had seemed to have been preparing a particularly selected psychopathic team to take us on when we became integrated. The rules were a closely guarded secret between the rugby master and his team. The game started and someone threw me the ball. I started to make my way towards the opposition but a group of them came hurtling towards me. They seemed intent on getting the ball and so I threw it in the air and stepped aside. The whistle then blew and the psycho master explained that we would restart from where I received the ball and that I was to keep hold of it and run towards the opposition touch line. Everyone returned to their original positions and the whistle blew. I was again passed the ball and before I had progressed a couple of steps was promptly steamrollered into the mud. I was quite fit having worked on the farm and provided it was a non-contact sport could hold my own against the best in long jump, high jump, 100 yards and 220 yards but I failed miserably at rugby and football. My sports kit consisted of hand-me-down clothes and I was often castigated by the sports teacher for looking scruffy.

During the early years of my Grammar school life my brother John had got married to Sally Tucker. The Tucker family had a large farm at East Prawle on the coast. The family consisted of John and Molly Tucker and their children Sally (eldest), William, Roger, John, Robin and Jane. John had attended school with Sally who was in a year above him. When she left school she was commandeered to work on the farm although she had always aspired to be a teacher. The wedding took place at Kingsbridge Catholic church on October 6th 1962 with a reception at West Charlton Village Hall. John was at that time working for Uniroyal in Edinburgh and after the wedding Sally went back to Edinburgh with John to live in a flat in Marchmont Road. My Mum and I did visit them when I was about 13 and I remember going through Sheffield on the train and being amazed at how glum and smoky it looked.

During my last year at school, I had also progressed to motorised transport and had bought a second-hand Panther 250cc motorbike from someone in Cornwall. It was a nice-looking bike but not very reliable and suffered badly from oil leaks like most British bikes of the time. I spent a lot of time trying to keep it roadworthy which was partially the reason that I went for my driving test three times before I passed.

At this time my father was helping out on a local farm called Lixton, owned by the Harris family. They had three sons – Roger, Trevor, and Graeme. Roger was a year older than me, and Trevor and Graeme were twins and a year younger. Roger had a workshop on his farm and the both of us became good friends through tinkering with motorbikes and cars. We remained good friends until he sadly died of a heart attack in March 2020.

My disappointing GCSE results meant that I would not stay on for A levels and it became a bit of a quandary as to how I could progress in life. I had little interest in farming apart from the mechanical side.

My brother John had done well at school, staying on for his A levels where he passed chemistry, physics and maths and became head boy. He went on to study rubber technology at Holloway Road, London where he obtained the equivalent of a degree.

Chapter 3

Education and Employment

*I*n 1965 John came to my academic rescue and had a meeting with the school head, and it was decided that perhaps re-sitting my GCSEs in another environment may be worth a try. I was then enrolled into Torquay Technical college to retake my O levels with an engineering bias. To begin with I stayed with my Aunt Beat and Uncle Jim in Newton Abbot and travelled to college each day from there by bus. After a month or so I found a room with the Luscombe family in St Efrides Road, Torquay which was quite close to the college. I shared a downstairs room with a guy called Alan from Seaton who was studying business. The family were very good to us. They had a son called Michael and a daughter called Elizabeth. Mr Luscombe worked at an abattoir and so we consequently did OK for meat. Mrs Luscombe was a very thin, active lady who smoked rather a lot and was a member of the local rowing club. At the time my parents still ran the farm and so I returned home on my Francis Barnett 250cc motorbike each Friday evening, returning on Sunday evening.

Our main home at the college was not in the main building, but in an old house called Hess Bank situated opposite the Grammar school entrance. We were a rather ragbag group of students coming from two directions. Ones like me who had shot for the moon and missed, and ones who had dropped off their perch but somehow bounced back up. There were all boys in our group which perhaps helped us to focus on our work and after a year I emerged with four O levels of a respectable grade. It was suggested that I should stay on at college and study for the OND (Ordinary National Diploma) in engineering.

During this first year at college, I picked up with a guy called Alan Perryman. He was on the same course but in a different group. Alan was a keen member of the College Youth Theatre Workshop. He said that lots of girls go along to it, and they were all a bit 'way out'. The group was run by a lady called Jo Tennent, whom I rather liked. I had never before considered any theatrical inclination but in Alan's case it seemed like engineering and drama could cohabit. He looked a bit 'dramatic' as he always wore stripey trousers to college which seemed a bit whacky to me. I found that I quite enjoyed drama. It combined escapism from the day-to-day academic world, plus mixing with other students, mainly girls, who seemed easy to talk to. Most of what we did in the first year was improvisation, but it gave me confidence to understand how I might react in unfamiliar situations.

In my second year at college, I moved accommodation farther down St Efrides Road to the parents of Mrs Luscombe whom I had previously lodged with. I can't remember the reason why I moved but I think it was because they were refurbishing the house. Her parents were called Mr and Mrs Crocker or 'the Crocs' as all the lodgers called them. I had my own room and there were two other lodgers. One from Chagford called Guy who was studying business and wanted to be an auctioneer, and another who wanted to be a chef. Living here seemed a little more formal than the previous accommodation but they looked after us well and were active members of the TOADS (Torbay Operatic and Dramatic Society).

There seemed to be pressure put on the college drama group that they should produce a play to show what they were capable of. The Crucible by Arthur Miller was chosen and we began rehearsals. I was allocated the minor part of Giles Corey but I gave it my all and enjoyed playing the part. My friend Alan took the lead role of John Proctor. The Crucible is a satirical play about witchcraft and is based on the McArthur communist hunt. Miller wrote the play as an allegory for McCarthyism. The rehearsals were quite intense, but we were determined to put on a good show. At the end of the first night, we were all taken aback as none of the audience applauded. The Crocs had duly attended that first night and they were still in tears when I got back after the show. I said we were disappointed that no one had applauded, and they said that the atmosphere the play created would have been broken by the audience applauding. I can still hear the girls screaming during the court scene, they certainly didn't hold back.

During this time at college, I joined the sub-aqua club. It was run by the technical drawing lecturer called Mr Harwood. He was a small, dapper sort of chap and quite easy to get on with. It had little or no equipment at the time and in the evening meetings we were employed in making our own wet suits. The club had a small inflatable dinghy with an outboard motor. When we had completed our suits we went down to try them out at Beacon Cove in Torquay. We only had snorkels as the college had yet to purchase breathing equipment. We climbed aboard the dinghy and went out about 200 yards from the beach where we jumped into the water. I never liked this initial part of diving as the cold water slowly seeps into your suit and gives a kind of creepy feeling. The water was about 20 feet deep. John Wreford, the dinghy driver, then went away from the group. The idea being that he would return when we were ready to scramble back on board. We duly bobbed about for a while and I decided to see if I could swim down to the bottom. I swam down but as I was coming back up I could hear the sound of an outboard motor approaching. I was out of air and so had to continue my way to the surface. Just as I surfaced the front of the dinghy hit me and rode over me. I could see the propeller coming towards me and managed to grab the side of the boat and get my head above the water. The boat was still moving forward and my legs started to drift up to the propeller. My legs went past the propeller, but my right thigh hit it. At that point the people in the boat realised I was there and cut the engine. The propeller had cut through my suit, some of which was now wrapped around it. I was cut free and hauled into the boat expecting to see some serious damage to myself as I knew that I had been hit. Fortunately, the wet suits we had made were from heavy industrial neoprene which was twice as thick as a standard suit. All I had to show for my encounter was two weal marks across my thigh with some heavy bruising. I called a halt to sub-aqua after that.

The OND course was what was called a sandwich course, whereby we were to spend six months at college and then six months in industry before going back to college for the final six months. Many on the course were sponsored by their employers and so had a workplace to go to. I was not sponsored and had to find an engineering company that would take me for the experience. The head of department announced that there was a vacancy with a company called Watermota at Abbotskerswell near Newton Abbot. They apparently converted Ford engines for marine use and were in the old Whiteway's Cider factory. Outside of the factory was a conventional brick-built house that acted as the offices and a huge tower that held up a square prefabricated steel water tank. The tank had once carried the Whiteway's logo but this had now been replaced by the Watermota sign. The Ford engine conversions sounded good to me as I had an E93A Ford Popular which required regular fixing. I went for the interview and met the MD who was called Aubrey Denton. He was extremely well spoken and drove an E-Type Jaguar. He asked if I had any marine experience. I said that I had gone to the Isle of Wight on the ferry with my Mum when I was about 14 to visit my aunt and uncle. That seemed to be sufficient experience to get me the job. I then had to find some accommodation. In the 1960s this was not too difficult as several families took in lodgers. I found accommodation in the centre of Abbotskerswell with the Wakeham family. The house was a big old Devon longhouse with a large yard and orchard. Mrs Wakeham was a jolly, short, rather rotund woman whom we nicknamed Mrs Wobbly. Her husband was called Reg and drove a grey MiniVan. They had a son, David, who was a builder and a daughter, Pam, who ran a small farm. The house was quite dark inside but had a big open fire in the living room where we used to congregate before dinner. At this time, I remember in particular two other lodgers. There was Bob the baker, who looked just like Danny Kaye, and Lenny who drove a JCB and had an open top mark 2 Ford Zodiac. Lenny was about 25 and tall and tanned with long blonde hair. He kept himself to himself but apparently was very successful with the young Swedish female language students who came to Torquay in the summer. Bob was about 45 years old and delivered bread around the Torbay area. He started very early in the morning but equally finished early and so he was always at home when I finished work. Bob always seemed happy and he was fun to talk to. He had been in the navy and married but divorced. He was in a rather unusual relationship with a married woman from Torquay. Her husband knew of the relationship but seemed unperturbed by it. We would all collect in the front room before dinner and watch The Magic Roundabout. After dinner we would sometimes watch Crossroads and offer the cast 'advice'.

At Watermota I was viewed somewhat suspiciously by some of the shop floor workers as I was not really a true employee and could be a management spy. I was put to work assembling water pumps with an older guy called Ron. Ron was OK to me and quite jovial. My work bench was quite near to the engine test bay wherein lay my nemesis by the name of Fred Froom. Fred was a few years older than me and would have perhaps been in his early twenties. He was a stocky guy with black curly hair and was somewhat the 'Cheeky Chappy' of the shop floor. Although I had to work alongside him, Fred would never speak to me. This went on for several weeks until one day the ice broke. We used to play a sort of game of cricket some lunchtimes in one of the empty adjoining warehouses. If the bowler got the batsman out he would then take over as batsman, there only being one wicket. If the batsman was caught out, the catcher would become batsman. It provided quite a fast, interesting game. I was batting and Fred was bowling. As it was me batting Fred was giving it 120 per cent. After several unsuccessful bowls, Fred suddenly decided I was out. A cry went up that I was not out but Fred would hear none of it and approached me to take the bat. "Gimmee the effing bat," he said. I refused and held on to it and Fred stood in front of me demanding the bat. I then threw the bat down and walked up face to face with Fred. The whole warehouse went quiet and I don't know why I said it but the words came out, "Do you want to push it, Fred?" Fred replied, "Nah," and walked back into the works. After that incident we became good friends and often went swimming at Penn Inn swimming pool during our lunch hour together. A further outcome of my confrontation with Fred was that I was befriended by a guy of about the same age as me called Dave Pugh. Dave was the 'village boy' and knew everyone and everything that went on in Abbotskerswell. He worked some evenings at the Kingskerswell dog track. He told me there was a vacancy there helping out for a couple of evenings a week if I was interested. It was ten shillings a night with a cup of tea and a bun thrown in. I went to the track with him and met Charlie who ran the show there. He was a typical dog track owner with pork pie hat and a coat with a fur lined collar (think Arthur Daley). The work was pretty easy, consisting of either jumping over the fence between races and raking the sand on the corners or helping to feed the hare wire back into its pulleys. The hare in those days was operated by a wire which was pulled around the track. The hare was pulled by a car engine and gearbox situated in the middle of the circuit. The operator would accelerate or decelerate the engine in order to keep the hare just ahead of the hounds. At the end of each race the hare and wire had to be pulled back around the track. Danny Broadway was the 'heavy' who did this job as it was quite difficult to pull, especially on the second circuit. Danny was followed by one of us who had a pole with a hook on the end which we used to clip the wire over the pulley. Danny was a quiet guy and looked as though he came from a Romany background. He always wore a red neckerchief, was about late twenties and had black curly hair. Ten shillings a night plus a cup of tea and a bun plus a few laughs seemed quite a good way to spend an evening. The track was very close to the main train track running from Newton Abbot to Paignton. One evening during a race a rabbit appeared on the track. The hounds saw the rabbit and naturally went in hot pursuit. The rabbit made its escape across the railway line followed by the hounds and several owners. Fortunately, no trains appeared, and the hounds were recaptured and peace was eventually restored. I expect that story has been related down the local rabbit generations. One day Charlie hit on an idea to make more money by charging for parking at the site. He told me that I would now be responsible for collecting the car park money. This didn't appeal to me at first as it meant standing in the car park on my own and away from the action. As the punters left their cars and paid me the parking charge, they would often ask me for a race tip. I hadn't really followed the dogs, but one day I guessed and recommended a dog to a punter. It actually won and at the end of the races the punter came over to me and gave me a large tip. From this I worked out a cunning plan. There were normally five or six dogs in a race. If I recommended each dog in turn to subsequent punters, each race would result in me having a one in five or six chance of picking a winner. This resulted in more tips plus some abuse from the punters who had taken my tip and lost but at the end of the day I was up.

It was always worth me taking a walk through the kennels, though, before a race as you could sometimes catch a dog owner force feeding their dog a banana. A lot of banana gives a dog severe indigestion. If you have had a dog that is consistently winning the odds in a small track become heavily stacked against it and so it is important that it occasionally loses. Bananas were good because they don't show up in a drugs test. If I saw the banana trick being pulled, I knew not to recommend that dog.

I kept up with the college drama group during my time at Watermota. I was selected to perform a play with a girl called Sue Futrell. The play was called Lovers and was written by Brian Friel. It was the story of Joe and Mag, two young Irish teenagers who lived on a large housing estate. Mag had fallen pregnant by Joe and the two were due to be married after their school exams for which they are revising during the play. We performed it outside on the lawn of the college campus and it obtained very successful reviews.

Returning to college after my work experience at Watermota I started to find the lectures rather challenging especially the maths which had never been my strong point. I returned to the farm to await my results but already knew that I had failed.

Whilst awaiting my results, which was around March time, I took a job with an agricultural contractor called Colin Janes. He operated from a yard in the small village of Modbury. I had always been interested in the mechanical side of farming and this seemed my chance to get involved in it. I first went for a chat with Colin who was a man in his mid-thirties, about 5' 8" tall with blonde hair and a ruddy complexion. He was very much a 'Devon Boy' and always looked somewhat anxious. He offered me a job and I started almost right away. I met the rest of the team who although reasonably friendly looked a rather rough bunch, some of whom I recognised from fights in local dance halls. One of them introduced me to the company motto which was 'Thou shalt not stop!' They didn't either, and would press on through any conditions. Colin's area that he covered stretched from Tavistock in the north to Salcombe in the south. Roaring around the country on tractors in the spring and summer was great fun. We were paid seven shillings an hour and it was important to get as many hours in as and when you could because when it rained, we got sent home. Most of the tractors didn't have cabs and so we had to dress according to the weather. Colin's main tractor was the Nuffield 4/65 of which he had three. This tractor was fast on the road and so reduced travelling time. It was though extremely dangerous on steep ground, but more of that later. The line up also included a Ford Super Six, a Roadless 75, a six-cylinder Fordson Super Major six-cylinder conversion, a Massey Ferguson 178 Multi Power and a David Brown 990. Starting in March meant that muck spreading was high on the agenda. The normal line up was two Nuffield's with Howard Rotaspreaders and one Nuffield with a rear end loader. I was normally assigned to spreading. One day we were sent to a farm at Peter Tavy. The farm was mainly a dog breeding centre with some beef stock. All the outhouses seemed to be filled with dogs and puppies. The farm was a typical Dartmoor farm, consisting of grey stone walls covered in a lot of moss. The place looked rather depressing and had a large pile of manure in the centre of the yard which we were tasked to clear. We were shown which fields we had to spread and set to work. On about my second trip out to the field I started spreading and saw some large lumps flying out of the spreader. I stopped the tractor and went back to investigate. The large lumps turned out to be pieces of dog. I didn't know what I should do and so continued spreading. I met the other driver going out to the field and told him about it. He said, "I know, wait till you get back to the yard." When I got back to the yard, Terry, who was driving the loader, was being sick from the smell, and had tied a scarf around his face. We pressed on through the day and eventually cleared the mass animal grave. The finished field looked like something from a battle, with bits of dog and calf scattered all over it. We thought we had finished, but no, he had a pile of dried slurry in the next field for us to spread. This slurry had come from a sewage works. It was easy to spread but when we had finished the field was covered in condoms.

    When the manure spreading season came to a close we moved on to cutting silage. A similar set up, with one cutting and two draying the cut silage back to the farm. There was also another job involved which required a tractor with a buck rake to transport the silage deposited at the base of the silage stack up to the top of it. I was often allocated this job as I seemed to quite good at getting the tractor to climb up the stack. I was working on a stack at a farm owned by the Granger family near St Anne's Chapel. The silage was coming in thick and fast and I was building the stack up using a Nuffield 4/65 with a buck rake and no cab. The stack had reached the end of the building and I had no choice but to keep increasing the steepness of it by keeping enticing my 'Nuffy' to keep scrambling backwards up to the top to deposit each load. It was becoming increasingly difficult to sit in the seat on the face of the pile when suddenly the tractor started a strange rolling motion. I knew it was tipping over but had no chance to abandon ship. Suddenly everything went dark and very quiet. I thought I was dead, as I couldn't hear or see anything. I then heard some muffled shouting and managed to start to move my limbs. I scrabbled around and emerged up into the sunlight. Some people came and pulled me out and brushed me down. It was a hot day and I had been working without a shirt and could see no major injuries apart from having a rather sore back. The tractor had rolled down the silage clamp and ended up on all four wheels and set off across the field. Someone had run after it and managed to kill the engine. The two rear mudguards were crushed together over the driver's seat but apart from that the tractor seemed little damaged. I had somehow lost my shirt jacket in the accident and it was nowhere to be found. The other guys phoned Colin to tell him of the event. Colin didn't make much of it and didn't even come out to the farm. He sent out the workshop fitter to straighten out the mudguards and to put the wheels out wider. This can be achieved by jacking up the tractor, loosening the wheel bolts and adjusting the wheel positions. I was then put back on the tractor to finish the day's harvest. As evening closed in I started to get cold and the farmer gave me an old overcoat to wear which I travelled home in that evening. My Mum wanted to know where my shirt was and I made up an excuse that we had moved site that day and I had left it behind. I did tell my Dad though and he said to be careful in future. There did, however, become regular weekly 'events' of a health and safety nature. Partly from the type of drivers that were hired and partly from the type of work that farmers expected us to carry out. Any steep fields that needed tilling or reclaiming, they called in a contractor. I remember being sent to spread artificial fertiliser on a really steep field outside of Ermington using the David Brown. The tractor crabbed across the side of the hill and so I stood on the upper footplate not wishing to encounter another roll over. When I returned to the yard, Terry, who was always ready for a joke, said, 'You returned, then. We were all expecting to be going to a funeral next week.' In one day alone someone hit a hedge on the main road to Salcombe and tipped a Nuffield over. I was tasked with collecting the driver who had escaped injury, but just as I was leaving someone rolled in with a smashed up baler having hit a bridge with it. When I returned to the yard with the driver we were told that the combine harvester had tipped over in a field near Bigbury.

One day Colin told me to take the lorry, which was a ten-ton Thames Trader, and collect some bales. I said to Colin that I was only 19 and that you had to be 21 to drive a truck. His reply was that I had a driving licence and so I was more legal than a lot of the other buggers working there. The next surprise that Colin pulled on me was that he sent me with a John Deere track machine to dig out a site at a farm at Tigley. I had to meet the architect on site and he would lay out the levels where I was to dig. I met the architect and saw for the first time the John Deere. I walked around with him while he put posts in the ground and explained what he wanted done. He seemed intent on watching me start, but I explained that I was due my morning break, plus I had to put fuel in the digger and grease it. He seemed to get the message and left. I jumped on the machine and had a quick play with all the knobs and levers and worked out what moved what. Once I got moving, I found that I got the hang of it quite quickly. Colin turned up later in the day and seemed impressed with my work, or as impressed as Colin ever got. It was a crazy time but I, as a young, single guy, enjoyed it immensely. One evening we were out picking up bales until after midnight because Colin had promised to start a new site the next day. There were no mobile phones then and so I couldn't tell my Mum that I might be a bit late. Every day was different and there seemed no end to the crazy jobs we were given, from clearing old gravestones from a cemetery to trying to create a flower garden using a Super Six and getting it stuck in the lily pond. My best week for hours was 83. Even at seven shillings an hour I was earning quite a bit of money which was good because I was saving up to go to Mauritius. Why Mauritius? My brother John was now working there at a rubber processing factory he had set up in Port Louis with two Chinese guys. I had planned to travel as part of a package holiday in September. Package holidays in those days were somewhat odd, as you needed to belong to a specific group to book and travel on one. I seemed to remember suddenly belonging to a pigeon fanciers club to book my trip. The cost for two weeks including flights and hotel full board was originally quoted at £199. I went to the travel agent in Kingsbridge and booked my trip. As time drew on I heard nothing from the agent and not having a phone at home wasn't in a position to easily contact them. One day I was working with a Nuffield and flail mower clearing a particularly steep piece of gorse ground at a place called Long Lane in Kingston near Bigbury. The Nuffy was performing in its usual spectacular way in continually throwing its front wheels in the air whilst climbing the slope when my Mum suddenly appeared in the field. Having recovered from watching her son wrestling with a thoroughly bad-tempered Nuffield that seemed hell bent on self-destruction, she told me that the travel agent was going to cancel my trip to Mauritius as the price had risen to £240 and they assumed that at that price I would not want to go. The next day I had to take time off and visit the agent and pay the balance of the money. I was definitely going and wasn't risking life and limb driving tractors for no result. Taking time away was always a bad thing as on return you would get sentenced to bale-loading although it did command another six pence an hour.

 I obtained my first passport on 6th August 1969 at the age of 19 during my tractor driving time. On 31st August I set off from the farm on a bus to Plymouth railway station and from there took a train to Reading where I caught the bus to Heathrow. Air travel was a very relaxed approach in those days. You just rolled up at the airport with your ticket and passport and got on the aircraft with no security checks. The flight I took was a British Overseas Aircraft Corporation (BOAC) flight and the aircraft in question was VC10 – a very quiet aircraft with four engines mounted on the tail. I was a very nervous flyer and found it impossible to relax. I even found it difficult to eat and drink because of my anxiety. We left in the evening and experienced a very short night before the sun rose over the eastern skyline. There was a stop on the way, at Entebbe in Uganda. This was a rather unnerving experience because the airport staff there who boarded the aircraft were very aggressive and shouted instructions at the aircrew. I did not know at the time but the Idi Amin dictatorship was in its ascendancy and the security forces were on high alert. I was somewhat relieved when we took off and headed on our final leg to Mauritius. We landed on Monday, 1st September in the afternoon at a relatively small airport where I was met by my brother John and his wife Sally. By this time, they had twin daughters called Jane and Joanne who were born in Malaysia which is where John had worked for two years after leaving Edinburgh. He had been a rubber technologist working for the Malaysian government at the Rubber Research Institute in Kuala Lumpur. They took me to my hotel which was situated at a place called La Morne on the southwest of the island. I had a very nice room that opened out onto a sandy beach. The sea in front of the beach held a lagoon protected by a coral reef about 200 yards out, over which the sea continually crashed. The hotel was quiet and long-distance package holidays were still relatively new and the beach was largely deserted. The constant heat was something new to me. The summer of 1969 had been a good one at home and working outdoors for most of it, I had built up a bit of a tan. Here, though, there were no cool evenings, but there was a consistent breeze from the ocean that was refreshing. The next day John collected me from the hotel and took me to their house in Vacoas. The landscape was something I had never imagined. It was largely covered in sugar cane and volcanic boulders. There was the occasional large bulldozer working on clearing the large volcanic boulders to create more land to grow more sugar cane. There were also not so many cars as we travelled through the countryside, but several people on bicycles. John had a white Toyota Corolla car which, although small, was very well equipped and quite zippy. After about 30 minutes we arrived at the house. It was an old colonial style of house with a tropical garden and a large wooden garden shed where a gardener seemed to lurk. It struck me as reminiscent of drawings that I had seen in Rudyard Kipling books. It was there that I met my nieces Jane and Joanne for the first time. They were two years old and looked identical with both having blonde curly hair. The atmosphere was very relaxed and it was decided that I should stay at the hotel for the two weeks and then stay with John and Sally for two weeks, as it was possible to change my flight dates without penalty. John then took me to a small industrial estate in Port Louis where he had built the factory for processing rubber for tyres. The factory was called Rubber Industries. It was very clean and light inside and was probably about 3000 square feet in size. It had a rubber mixing mill and a Barwell hydraulic extruder. There were also some presses for manufacturing bicycle tyres. There were about three employees and the foreman was a young Mauritian who always wore a sailor's cap. That evening I went back down to the hotel in a Fiat 500 that John had somehow acquired for me. The next few days I spent swimming and sunbathing. The coral was amazing and looked as though it had small electric lights over it. I had never seen anything so spectacular underwater as my first few days swimming inside the reef. The hotel guests seemed to be all older couples, mainly from South Africa and so I was somewhat on my own, but I still found it very interesting and enjoyed the warmth and good food at the hotel. There was some occasional evening entertainment in the form of a disco or barbeque but mainly most people were happy to eat and sunbathe. These few relaxing days were very welcome to me after the full-on months that I had experienced as a member of the Janes gang. I didn't, though, appreciate how strong the sun was and after two days began to feel decidedly uncomfortable. My lips and nose had swollen and cracked, and my stomach and back were red raw. My hair had turned blond, and I could hardly bear any clothes to touch me. It took me quite a few days in the shade before I started to recover. I therefore went up to visit John and Sally on quite a few occasions while my body sorted itself out. I helped out as and when I could by running a few errands to get spare parts for the factory from suppliers in Port Louis. This was a fascinating place, with a heavy smell of spices in the warm air and several races of people who seemed happy in each other's company. There were African, Indian, Chinese, European and native Mauritians all wheeling and dealing along the dock area. I bought a very flashy looking watch from a street trader for around £1 and it did actually last me several years. The main language was French but most people used English. I met John's two Chinese colleagues. One owned a furniture store and the other owned a property business. They took us out for a meal in a Chinese restaurant in Port Louis which was situated on the waterside in the dock area. It was a somewhat downbeat restaurant but I always remember it as being one of the tastiest meals I had ever eaten. Time drifted by, and after my two-week stay at the hotel I moved in with John and Sally for my final two weeks. John had to travel to South Africa on business during this time and so I tried to make myself generally useful until his return. I left Mauritius on 29th September. On the way back I remember flying over the Middle East oilfields with their many flares lighting up the evening sky. We stopped off to refuel in Iran before continuing our journey back to Heathrow. I returned to the farm and tried to figure out what I could do next.

    I asked if Watermota would take me back which they seemed happy to do and allowed me to do a day release course back at South Devon Tech. The course I took was called a City and Guilds T3, and because of my OND experience I sat the exam in December 1969 and attained a pass with credit. I then progressed to the T4 stage whilst still on day release. I had moved back into the Devon longhouse and was once again well looked after by 'Mrs Wobbly'. This time, though, I had to share a room with another guy called Richard who was slightly younger than me and worked at Totnes Car Museum restoring old cars. He also went home at the weekend and like me returned on Sunday evenings. He was tall with thick black hair and rather large lips. A quiet lad, except when he returned on Sunday evenings and was often completely spaced out. One Sunday when he returned I was in bed. He came into the room and got into the wardrobe and went to sleep. I looked out of our window and saw his green Morris 1000 van with the engine still running and the lights on. I got dressed, went downstairs and switched off the lights and engine, came back up and put him to bed. He would never mention where or what he did on Sunday evenings. The attic room that we shared was rather cold in winter but absolutely stifling on summer nights when the sun had shone on the slate roof all day. The house had an apple orchard wherein lived a donkey called Shamus. He had apparently been purchased for Mrs Wobbly's granddaughter, but she took little interest in him. One summer evening, looking for something to do, I asked if I could take him for a ride. "Good luck," was the reply. I found Shamus in his stable quietly munching some hay. I jumped on his back and shouted the customary, 'Giddy up,' but he just stood still munching his hay. I climbed off his back and put on his bridle and dragged him protesting to the top of the orchard. I jumped on his back and he took off. I hung on and he headed straight back into the stable, nearly decapitating me in the low doorway. OK, I thought, let's try that again only this time with the stable door closed. We went off up to the top of the orchard once more and I again jumped on his back. Once again Shamus took off like a rocket heading for the stable but discovered the door was shut. He then tried to turn and bite my legs but I kept his head straight with the reins. He stopped for a moment and then took off again. I thought he had at last given in, but no, he had a cunning plan. He headed to the bottom of the orchard to where there were some low branches under which he dived, and I was forced to abandon ship. He calmly walked back to the stable and waited at the door. I went back and opened the stable door, took off his halter and wished him goodnight.

Chapter 4

Exmouth

My time at Watermota once again lapsed into a routine of day release at college, working at the dog track and theatre workshop. On weekends I still filled in with the Janes gang. My work at Watermota varied between working in the drawing office and filling in on the shop floor either machining or assembly. Aubrey Denton, the MD at Watermota, was always very good to me and encouraging but I felt I somehow didn't fit in any more. At home on the farm one Saturday morning I saw an advertisement in the Western Morning News job vacancy column for a Technical Assistant to the Technical Manager at a company called Swifts of Exmouth. I wrote off and was granted an interview. I had to take some time off work to attend the interview and so I called in sick and set off for Exmouth. Swifts were manufacturers of compression and injection moulded products of which I knew nothing. I had, however, had a hands-on chance about a week beforehand to get acquainted with some of the machinery used. My brother John and family had returned to live back in the UK. He had started a business buying and selling used rubber processing machinery. The previous weekend I had been helping him to take some presses out of a factory in Harpenden and noted some of the manufacturer's details. I remember that my interview was around lunchtime at the Swifts factory. It was a modern low level building situated in Pound Lane. I was in good time for the interview and after making myself known at the reception I was told to take a seat in the waiting area. I was very hungry and had brought a Mars bar with me which I started to eat. Halfway through eating it, I was told that someone was on their way to take me for the interview. I quickly gobbled the remaining bar and a gentleman in his early thirties appeared and introduced himself as Philip Anthony the technical manager. We shook hands and he took me to his office. The office was quite small and measured probably about 10 feet square. He showed me some of the products they made and asked me how I would calculate the volume of plastic in a cup. I think I gave some sort of answer about working it out in sections or alternatively putting it in a full container of water and measuring the displacement. I explained that I knew something about compression moulding presses and rattled off a few names which seemed to impress him. After the interview he took me back down the corridor but stopped off on the way at another room where he introduced me to Mr Caudrelier who was the owner. He was a short stout man in his fifties and smoked large Churchill type cigars. I called him 'sir' and said that I was pleased to meet him and was very impressed with the factory. I went back to the reception, shook hands with Philip Anthony, who said they would be in touch. Just before I left, I went into the toilet for a freshen up and when I looked in the mirror, I was horrified at what I saw. When I had rapidly eaten the Mars bar before my interview, a piece of the sticky inside had attached itself to the end of my nose. I therefore thought that I had blown my job interview. I waited for about a week being convinced that I had not got the job and contemplating my options when I received a reply which said I was successful and offered me the position of assistant to the technical manager. My next task was to try to find some accommodation. I was recommended to contact a family called Mudge. I visited them and met Ronald and Margaret Mudge. They were both in their thirties and had two daughters and lived at the end of a cul-de-sac called Booth Way. The house had three bedrooms but the room that I was shown was downstairs off the hallway and seemed very private and next to the downstairs toilet. Ron worked for Devon County Council as a time and motion study officer. The arrangement was that I would arrive on a Sunday night and depart back home on Friday after work. I went to work on the Monday and met Philip Anthony, my new boss who was the technical manager. He was now much more relaxed and jovial than he had been at the interview and welcomed me and showed me my desk in his office. We walked around the factory and saw the products that they manufactured, and I was introduced to various managers, all whose names I immediately forgot. The environment was completely alien to me, never having been in a plastics factory before. It was quite warm, all the presses being electrically heated. The factory layout was split into sections. There was compression moulding of melamine, injection moulding of thermoset plastics, finishing lines manned by benches of women, a toolroom and the warehouse and dispatch department. The whole factory employed something over 100 people.

Besides my small desk I also had a drafting board and I would spend most of my future time at Swifts working on this. Our main clients at that time were the NHS, BEA (British European Airways), BOAC (British Overseas Aircraft Corporation) and Harrods. Although the company was relatively small it had a very impressive client list which was mainly due to an excellent salesman called Stuart Sansom. I dropped in to working with Philip quite easily and found him to be a good mentor. The mould design, although at first appearing to be quite complicated, followed a pattern for sizes and tolerances, and after a couple of months I could work on designing a mould from scratch. Although our toolroom was quite capable of carrying out mould modifications they did not have the machines to efficiently produce moulds from scratch. This was subbed out to Torbay Tool and Gauge or Torbay Engineering.

One day when things in the office were quiet, I was asked by Philip Anthony if I would like to take on an extra role. The job entailed the setting of the shop floor work rates. The factory ran a piece work system whereby there was a basic wage per hour enhanced by how many products you produced. I felt very honoured by being offered, what seemed like, a very prestigious job at the age of 21. I was given a board with a stopwatch and paper with grid lines to record the operator's performance. I was told to assess the operator at what I considered to be a normal speed for which they are given the standard hourly rate of pay. Any increase in their production rate over this set performance would result in a higher pro rata rate of pay. That is, twice the set amount, then twice the hourly payment. This all seemed quite straight forward. I started off in the melamine moulding section watching the guys moulding the melamine pellets into cups, saucers plates, etc. I quickly noticed a few 'wrinkles' that they were working when I was observing them. They would pass the melamine pellets from one hand to another when loading the press or have the prewarming pellet microwave oven pushed a little way away from where they stood so that they had to take a step forward and backwards, thus losing time. I coped with these eventualities quite well in assessing the speed at which they could really work. Most of the moulding cycle time was based on the set cycle of the press and so it wasn't difficult to establish a work rate. I thought that I had mastered the production time and motion study until I was asked to assess the women on the moulded products finishing line. I started off in the same way as previously watching a selected operator spinning a plate to remove the flash. She was working at a very quick rate, probably about ten plates a minute which seemed impressive. I decided that she was probably working a little faster than I would assess normal, and so allocated time and a quarter for the rate. I reported the rate back to Bert Mabin, the production manager who was in charge of collecting the production records. The next day a very agitated Bert Mabin burst into my office and asked how I had assessed the plate finishing production as the whole team of women on the line were now on quadruple time. I rushed out into the factory to see the women spinning four plates at a time instead of the one plate that I had timed. I called a halt and reset the rate to four times my normal. I went back out the next day only to be collared by one of the women to say that she could not keep up the same speed as the others. I said that was unfortunate but perhaps with practice she would get faster. I then got the folded arms treatment where she announced that she was pregnant and had to make frequent visits to the toilet and that the firm was penalising her for being pregnant. What I thought had been a very prestigious part of my job rapidly became a nightmare and I could understand why no one else wanted to do it.

Whilst living in Exmouth I continued with my interest in the theatre and joined The Young Northcott. The Northcott Theatre was a new style of 'In the Round' theatre. The Young Northcott (YN) met each week in an old house in Northernhay Street, Exeter. The building had been an actual house in its day and probably dated from Victorian times. Downstairs was an entrance hallway leading into a large room with the wall painted black and in which we rehearsed. Upstairs was a chill out area for coffee with some comfortable tatty furniture. The *front door to the property was ordained with a lead glazed window. We did mainly theatre workshop type of stuff until it was decided that we should put on a performance at the Northcott Theatre itself. The play which was chosen was The Diary of Anne Frank; I played Mr Kugler although in Anne Frank's diaries she called him Mr Kraler. He was the owner of the house that sheltered the Frank family. The Northcott were very keen on the actors actually living the role and so the whole cast spent the weekend in the attic of the Northernhay House. We went in on Friday evening and emerged again on Sunday evening. I think we did one matinee and one evening performance and I seem to remember that both houses were full. We also did some theatre workshop away weekends at various outreach centres such as Beaford in North Devon and Pixies Holt on Dartmoor. The early seventies were a great time for Flower Power and enjoying a new sense of freedom.*

One evening while we were rehearsing there was a resounding crash in the hallway. We ran out and saw a large rock on the carpet and the front door glass panel smashed. Outside everything seemed quiet and so another guy and I walked out into the garden but saw no one. It was a very foggy evening, and the silence was somewhat eerie. We then walked out of the side gate into the street and saw a person shuffling off up the street. We ran after him and asked him if he had seen anyone throw the rock through the window. He was a man, I guessed, in his forties, with a trilby hat and raincoat. He said that he hadn't seen anyone and started to get agitated. I asked him if he was sure, as it had caused a lot of damage. Because he was denying it, there was not much we could do, and so turned to walk back to the building. It was then that I felt an arm around my neck and although he was a big guy, I somehow rolled him over my shoulder and fell on top of him on the ground. I managed to keep him down, but he then burst into tears and pleaded for me not to hurt him. Fortunately, our drama coach had phoned the police and they arrived within a matter of minutes and took him away. Later, I had to go to the police station to give a statement. They were very keen to know if I had punched him and that was why he fell over; I got the impression that it wouldn't have looked good for me if I had. It turned out that he had only recently been released from the local mental hospital and after my statement I heard no more about it.

I was still returning home to the farm at weekends and Dad, being in his early seventies and suffering from arthritis in his hips, decided it was time to sell the farm. Neither my brother John nor I had shown any real interest in farming, but Dad was quite philosophical about it. He said that what he had always wanted was to have his own farm and he had done it. It was now up to us to make our own way.

The farm was put on the market and sold to the Hayman family.

Mum and Dad bought a small bungalow in Newton Abbot and left the farming life. It was a new life for them, and they seemed for once to be relaxed in each other's company. Leaving the farm for the last time was very sad. I had been working away from home a lot, but it always seemed to be a tranquil escape from the real world where nothing could touch you. I would miss the evening stroll around the farm with my gun, picking up a pigeon or pheasant. I would also miss the trips to the tidal River Avon at Aveton Gifford where I caught grey mullet on the incoming tide.

The bungalow was in Mayflower Avenue, detached, and looked across to a pine wood. It had a drive to the side but no garage. To the rear was a garden. Dad bought a prefabricated garage which was delivered, assembled, and erected. It was of quite a sturdy design and of a good solid construction which was just as well considering the future abuse that it would receive at my hands. From this garage I would start a small weekend sideline.

I had been through a range of cars at this time having passed my test in February 1967. I took the test in Dad's A35 van and passed first time. I remember there was snow on the ground and when we came back to the test centre the examiner told me to park anywhere. I looked along a line of parked cars and saw one small space which looked very slightly longer than the van. I managed to squeeze the van in first time and without hitting the pavement. Dad was somewhat reluctant to let me keep borrowing his van and quite rightly too. Since I had joined the college Karting Club I had become somewhat adventurous in testing out my cornering skills. My first car was a Ford Popular E93A which had the nickname of the 'Perpendicular Popular'. I bought it from John Buswell who was on the O level course with me at college. He had used it for hill-climbing trials and so it was kitted out with roll bars. The engine was a 1272cc side valve with a two-bearing crank. Henry Ford didn't believe in wasting metal if he could get away with it. The problem with a two-bearing crank is that when you soup up the engine the crank starts to whip and then snaps. In my first year with that car I replaced four engines! I then moved on to a Ford 100E van. My Mum asked me to take a mattress to the tip one day and so I put it in the back of the van. I never took it to the tip as it created rather a good courting vehicle! My next vehicle was a Mk2 Ford Zodiac. It was a lovely car in green and cream. It was rather thirsty and so I used to mix paraffin with the petrol. It did make the exhaust fumes smell rather suspicious and so to disguise this I added a small amount of Castrol R to the fuel mix. Those of you who have smelt Castrol R from an exhaust will be familiar with its hypnotic smell. After this car I then moved on to a Ford Anglia 105E 1200cc. It had a V-shaped dent in the radiator grill where the previous owner's wife had hit a telegraph stay wire. I replaced the radiator and it was a very comfortable economical car until the engine started to burn oil. I was familiar with Ford engines of this type having worked on them at Watermota. I decided to buy an exchange engine from a company in Dagenham, advertised in Exchange and Mart. There were a lot of companies in the Dagenham area who specialised in reconditioned Ford engines. My brother John was travelling up to this area over a weekend to look at some machinery. He had a Mini Traveller at the time. I was on holiday and I took the engine out of the Anglia and put in in a big travel trunk that we had at home. We drove up to London and while John was dealing with the machinery I went and exchanged my engine for a rebuilt replacement. The factory was a somewhat backstreet ramshackle affair but the guys there were helpful and knowledgeable. John had to stay on in the London area and so I came back on the train with my engine in the travel trunk which I manhandled into the luggage rack. When we got to Newton Abbot I pulled the trunk off the train. I stood looking for a trolley when a porter appeared around the corner. I asked him for a hand with my trunk and he went to pick it up and having got it about three inches off the round promptly put it down, asking what the hell I had got in it. We both manhandled it onto a trolley and via the lift got it to the station entrance. Definitely worth all of the 50p I gave him as a tip. I then got a taxi home with a similar comment from the taxi driver. I put the engine in the car the next day using the garage my Dad had bought and using a chain hoist I had acquired from somewhere fixed to the cross bar of the garage roof. I had some problems getting the engine started and it seemed to be that when they had fitted the valves in the cylinder head, they had cut the seats and the valves but hadn't ground them in. I lapped the valves in and reassembled the engine and it ran as sweet as a nut. I did a lot of miles with that engine, and it never let me down once. Having carried out this engine transplant and now having all the gear, I thought that perhaps I could set up a small weekend business. The problem was how to send the engines up to Dagenham and pick up a replacement. The answer was surprisingly right under my nose. Swifts where I was working had a delivery lorry that took parts for sewing machines to its sister company in Dagenham. I knew the driver quite well and he seemed to make one delivery a week up and back. I got chatting to him and it seemed he drove past the engine reconditioning factory. He agreed that for a fee he could take an engine up and bring one back. I advertised in the local paper my engine 'exchange over a weekend' service and was pleased to receive some enquiries. The system worked well. I had acquired a spare engine which I sent back with Dick the lorry driver and he would bring another one back and tip me the nod, and I would take my car around to his truck and put the replacement engine in the boot. When I went home on Friday evening a customer would drop their car around. I would have my tea and ably assisted by my Dad would get their car in the garage and I could have the engine out in an hour. Saturday would see me getting the new engine installed and the valves lapped in and on Sunday morning the customer would collect the car and pay me. The following weekend the customer would return and I would retorque the cylinder head and adjust the tappets. I found that I could make more money over the weekend than I made at Swifts during the week. I had the system set up and I never had a problem with any of the engines that I replaced. After a while Mum decided she didn't really like the bungalow any more as the surrounding fir tree woods made her feel tired. The property was put on the market, and they moved to a small, terraced cottage in Kingskerswell. There was no garage to this property and so I had to close my engine replacement sideline.

Whilst wandering around Exmouth one evening, I bumped into a guy called Dave Trehan whom I knew from my theatre workshop days in Torquay. He looked the part of a drama teacher, with thick curly hair and John Lennon type glasses. He said that he worked some evenings on the door at a nightclub in Exmouth which I think was called Samantha's, and to drop by. I duly rolled up there one evening and met Dave who let me in. I got a drink from the bar and went back to the door to talk to him. Dave was 'Mr Man about Town' and seemed to know several of the crowd – many of whom came from Rolle College, which was a teacher training academy. A girl he was talking to caught my eye. She was about the same height as me with long auburn hair and freckles and when she smiled her whole face seemed to light up. She said she was called Linda and was studying at Rolle College. I introduced myself and before I could say what I did, Dave said, "He plays for Exeter City football team." Linda seemed impressed by this and so I thought I would keep it going. We arranged to meet up for a drink the next week and I explained that I couldn't do weekends because we often played away. I had to do some quick swotting up on match fixtures for Exeter plus selecting a player who looked like me. I could explain away any name change by saying my friends called me by middle name so that I didn't get recognised in public. We met up again and seemed to hit it off. I told her a bit about the match, and she said she had thought she had seen me in the lineup in the paper. The football thing seemed to become less important as we enjoyed each other's company, and I eventually confessed, at which she didn't seem surprised. Linda and I were to stay together for about two years in a wild, passionate, and sometimes violent relationship. I think we were just too young to cope with our runaway emotions.

I became more and more involved with the design part of production at Swifts and fortunately less involved in the time and motion setting of piece work rates. I had an idea as to how we might make a two-colour melamine range without the need to use expensive colour foils that were bought in and had a limited shelf life. We made some prototype tooling and the two-part moulding system proved successful for which Swifts gained a patent and I got a 'Jolly well done'. Swifts had allowed me to continue my college studies and I had enrolled in a day release T6 Plant engineering course at Plymouth Poly. It was really run by the dockyard college that had been absorbed into Plymouth Poly.

It was a big old Victorian building next to the dockyard at Keyham. There were some of what might be described as the more street wise engineering brigade on the course all of whom seemed to be called Gordon. It was a two-year day release course dealing with the theory of boilers, compressors, turbines, etc. I passed the final exams gaining a distinction. I didn't know at the time, but this training would become very important to me for my future.

Swifts was really built around Stuart Sansom the sales manager. Stuart was a larger-than-life character in his thirties with tight-knit, black curly hair and an engaging manner. I was chatting with him in the car park one day after work and what Stuart said to me would stay with me for the rest of my life. I said to Stuart that I was impressed with his sales ability as it was really him that had built the company to what it was and I then said, "Stuart, you must be a bloody good talker?" He immediately looked me in the eye and said, "No, Richard, you're wrong, I'm a bloody good listener, that's what sells!" I always remembered that statement and it has always held true.

Chapter 5

Starting Bandvulc

*I*was beginning to get restless at Swifts and looking for a new opportunity when one day my brother John said he would like to have a chat with me about a business venture he was starting.

After moving back from Mauritius he had started a company called J. O'Connell & Associates which bought and sold used rubber processing machinery. As previously mentioned, I helped out sometimes during my holidays and weekends. This was the early 1970s, a time when British industry seemed to be in rapid decline and factories of all types were closing down, mainly because of poor management and lack of investment. Through his travels for the Malaysian Rubber Research Institute and also the factory he had helped set up in Mauritius, he had made many contacts to buy and sell machinery. He also had a Jewish contact in the Isle of Dogs in London who had a yard full of surplus rubber processing machinery. His name was Julius Borowitch, better known as Boris. Boris was the archetypal Jew, dressed in black with a black pork pie hat and drove a new Rolls-Royce. His office only had some basic furniture and when I went to visit with John he bought us lunch; a scotch egg each.

Boris had in his yard some old truck tyre retreading machinery and asked John if he wanted it. John had asked him how much he wanted for it and to his surprise Boris said, 'Nothing, just take it away. The two pieces of machinery were made by Karl Zangl of Germany and must have dated from the 1930s. They were basically a vertical cast iron gearbox that turned a hub which held a tyre by the beads. There was then an articulated arm which held a large motor with two spindles. Attached to these spindles was a rasp housing. The motor had two handles, similar to a motorbike, and the rasps were then guided across the tyre by the operator.

John had his promised chat with me one day and said that he was installing the retreading machinery in a building in Kingsbridge. The building was a coachwork called Tally Ho Coaches and was owned by a local entrepreneur Des Gullet. Des had a somewhat colourful history and could be considered a likeable rogue but did a lot of good work for the town. John explained that he thought there could be a good market for retreated truck tyres in the area. He had seen small companies in Malaysia and Mauritius carrying out the business and felt it was worth a go. I said that I had seen heart surgery on TV but that didn't encourage me to have a go at it. He said that he and Sally were prepared to put some money into the venture and if I came in I could have a third share in the company. I didn't have any commitments apart from my job at Swifts and so agreed to hand in my notice and start in the retreading business.

I moved into a room in John and Sally's house in Modbury. The house was called York House and was a three-storey terraced building which stood on a corner of Brownston Street and Back Street. Next door, down in Back Street, was the abattoir for the local butcher. Modbury was a small market town and across from York House there was actually a dairy farm right in the middle of the town. The farm was run by the Phillips family and twice a day they would drive the cows in from the fields and up the road to be milked. Modbury sat in the bottom of a valley and no matter which way you left you had to climb a hill. Around the back of York House was a yard where we could park cars and eventually store some tyres.

In between me working out my notice at Swifts, John had got a steam boiler, pipework, compressed air and two manually operated Laudisa tyre presses installed. The buffing machine that he had acquired from Boris was also wired in. We had a floor area of about 1,000 square feet on the second floor of the building. The floor was accessed by an earth ramp which went around the back of the building up to a sliding door. We were positioned just inside to the right of the door and the rest of the top floor was a car crash repair centre. The boiler was a second-hand vertical oil-fired type but it seemed capable enough of producing steam at 150 psi even though it had a large dent in its side.

Early days, each tyre lovingly hand finished!

The two tyre sizes that we were initially equipped to produce were 1000x20 and 900x20. At this time the majority of tyres were of crossply construction. That means they were made up of layers of fabric sandwiched between layers of rubber. We experimented by buffing off a couple of tyres but soon became overpowered by the smoke produced by the buffing blades. Also, the dust just fell on the floor and worryingly started smoking. Kicking it around to let it cool seemed to solve this problem. We decided that we needed some form of extraction system. We set off in our newly acquired second-hand BMC JU pickup truck to the local scrapyard. We acquired a large drum which was about six feet tall and two feet in diameter. We also found a large 'snail type' extractor fan. Pleased with our purchase we set about connecting up the fan and tank with a flexible hose. We cut a hole in the building sheeting and made an exhaust pipe. We also cut a small doorway at the bottom of the tank in order that we could remove the buffing dust into bags. When started, the whole ensemble created an encouraging noise and created a suitable suction at the buffing head. We now had a fully operational production buffing machine. Having buffed a tyre we now needed to rebuild one. This was achieved by using the body of the other buffing machine and mounting an arm with a roller and handle over the top of it. The rubber that we used was a long band of about twelve inches wide by about three quarters of an inch thick and tapered out at the edges. It was known in the trade as camelback because it had two slight humps where the shoulders of the tyre were situated. After buffing we would give the tyre a quick brushing to remove any surface dust and then paint over the buffed area with a rubber solution. John had acquired some camelback from a Chinese friend in Kuala Lumpur who had a retreading factory but also mixed his own rubber compounds. The camelback was very high in natural rubber which made it very springy. Often, we would wrap the tread around the tyre only to see it spring back off onto the floor. Adhesion could be aided by wiping solvent around it with a rag before rolling it down. This stained your hands black and dried out your skin. There was no way of washing it off and so we looked permanently like half made up minstrels. We did nothing to the sides of the tyres in those days, just leaving the original manufacturer's details on the side with the name 'Bandvulc' engraved in small letters on each shoulder of the tread. John invented the name Bandvulc. In the early seventies, anything that sounded British immediately had a bad reputation. It was a time of serious factory closures and redundancies with British products being looked on as inferior. There were two international franchised retreading companies at that time. An American company called Bandag and a German company called Vacuum Vulk. John came up with the name Bandvulc from this. It sounded better than O'Connell Retreads.

With our ad hoc machinery we managed to make about five tyres a day, mainly for local hauliers who did tipper and farm work. We did a few for longer distance trucks but they seemed to go bang which is not something tyres were meant to do. At the time of starting, the dual carriageway was being constructed from Exeter to Plymouth and there were several tipper trucks on the project mainly owned and operated by Indians and Irish. Word got out that we were retreading tyres at quite a cheap price and so we had a constant stream of battered cars and vans delivering and collecting tyres from us. We were starting to discover that tyres had to be round. They also needed not to be porous, which happened if we applied too little tread compound, or bumpy if we applied too much. This required investing in a tape measure. We were now starting to get technical with our manufacturing. The JU pickup was becoming somewhat of a liability. The engine wasn't really up to the job and burned out exhaust valves and blew head gaskets which I repaired in an evening or weekend.

The Laudisa tyre presses that we had relied on the total pressure of 200 psi being held in the tyre during moulding, by two very large side plates that were on wheels. These side plates were pushed into place on either side of the press and a large shaft of about four inches diameter slid through the two plates. This shaft had a large capstan-like nut that screwed onto the end of the shaft to keep the side plates in place against a pressure of some 60 tons. The threads had started to get weak and one day, just as I walked past, the presses of one of them stripped the threads and exploded. The side plates weighed about 200 kilos each. One flew through the air and hit a wardrobe that we kept our coats in, smashing it to matchwood, and one flew past me, hit and dented the building RSJ. The whole building shook violently. Fortunately, it was lunchtime and our small band of guys were sitting back out of the way. The shock wave, however, hit all of us and we couldn't eat or drink for a couple of hours; plus, we were all temporarily deafened by the explosion. There was a sudden crowd of visitors peering through the steam caused by the broken pipes as we scrambled to shut everything down. We had the large pin remade and drilled a hole across the bar at the end and secured it with a half-inch locking pin. We had no more problems after this.

The JU pickup was now not really fit for purpose with tyres often falling off the back of it and into the road. It was easy to tell when this had occurred as one could hear a squealing of brakes plus loud blaring horns. We then invested in a Bedford TK, bought from a dealer in Plymouth. It was a tidy little 4-cylinder truck. It looked as though it had never carried any heavy weights and was light blue in colour with a map of the south-west over the cab. It was a sign written with F.E. Harris on each side.

We kept meaning to paint out the signwriting but never seemed to get around to it. We also thought that it may be better to leave it as trying to blot it out might make it look rather tatty. Our customers kept commenting on the truck and the fact that it had belonged to F.E.Harris. One day I decided to ask someone why our truck seemed to be a source of amusement. I was asked, "Do you know who F.E.Harris is?" I said that I did not and was then told that he was the local coffin manufacturer. Retreaded tyres did not have a good reputation at that time and delivering them in an ex coffin truck did little for our reputation.

Not long after we had acquired the truck, a tyre building machine came up for sale in Aberdeen. We put in a bid for it which was accepted. It was at the premises of George Webster, quite a large retreader at the time. We thought it would be cheaper for me to drive to Aberdeen in the truck and inspect the machine and then load it and bring it back. Linda and I were still together at that point and she had always said she wanted to go to Scotland. We had little money for accommodation and so put a mattress and some bedding in the back of the truck and set off one Saturday morning. The truck travelled at little more than 50 mph but we made a layby in Kendal on our first evening. Having got some fish and chips we settled down for the night. It seems we had parked by a pavement that was the main way back from the pub for the locals, because all through the evening anyone who went past the truck instinctively banged on the side. Next morning we set off again. Just outside of Edinburgh we hit our first problem. As we neared a corner I took my foot off the throttle but nothing happened, we kept going at full throttle. I braked hard and kept hitting the throttle pedal to no avail. I then reached for the stop control which cut the engine, but when I pushed it in the engine began to race again. We managed to limp to a layby and stopped the engine. I checked all the throttle linkages but could find nothing amiss. We were stuck in the Highlands outside Edinburgh with no communication. I found I could start the engine but there was no control over the throttle other than by pulling and pushing the stop control. We decided to try to press on using this method. Along the open roads I found that I could just about control it but as we neared the city it became rather difficult and somewhat dangerous. So there we were, on a March Sunday afternoon in Edinburgh with a dying Bedford truck. We coasted into a bus stop and stopped the engine. It was about 3 pm. Linda then had a bright idea. She said that she had seen a transport yard not far back. I had not seen it as my eyes had been on stalks trying to wrestle with the stop control and the traffic. Linda said that she would go back to the transport yard and see if she could chat up someone to come to our aid. She was only gone about ten minutes, when she came running back excitedly saying that she had found someone. She said that she had spoken to Colin the owner and he was on his way to help. Colin, a guy in his thirties, very soon turned up and assessed the situation. "The diaphragm in the engine governor is broken," he stated. "Can't fix it today as we don't have the part, but you can leave it in the yard, and we will fix it first thing in the morning for ye." He then offered to drive us to a nearby hotel. We spent the night in the hotel marvelling at our good fortune to have found Colin. Next morning, we caught a bus back to the transport yard and true to his word, Colin had the Bedford up and running again by late morning.

We set off again, but as we crossed the Forth Bridge the red battery warning light came on indicating that the alternator had stopped charging. Thinking that Aberdeen was not much farther, and it was daylight, we decided to press on. Once we had crossed the bridge, we saw a sign that said 'Aberdeen 200 miles'. WHAT?! We soldiered on and by late afternoon found ourselves in Aberdeen on a piece of waste ground parking up for the night. Aberdeen in March is cold, especially when you are trying to sleep in the back of a truck with no heating. Next day broke bright and clear and we set off to find Websters Retreading factory. It was on an industrial estate and George Webster himself came to meet us. It was a big factory from what we had previously seen, but George was giving up retreading to concentrate on making rubber products for the oil industry. He later went bankrupt, so not a good choice. Should have stuck with the retreading, George. He showed us the machine which was a SIO tread builder and it was in very good condition. SIO was a well-known quality machine manufacturer based in Odense, Denmark. Everyone was very helpful, and they put it on a forklift and lifted it to go into the back of the truck. Problem number two; it was just too high to fit under the roller shutter door. I had a rather bad sinking feeling at that point! No matter, the good men of Scotland came up with a solution. They would remove the roller shutter, put the machine in the truck and refit it and that's what they did. We were soon on our way again and the battery seemed to be holding out. We had telephoned Colin to say that we would like to drop by again to get him to fix the alternator. We arrived at Colin's in the early afternoon and he quickly changed the alternator brushes and off we went once more. That night we made it to Carlisle and decided once again to stay in a small hotel as we were both tired and hungry.

By late the next evening we arrived back in Exmouth and I parked up the truck and spent the night at Linda's leaving next morning for Kingsbridge.

The machine proved to be a useful purchase and enabled us to build tyres much more accurately and quickly.

After a year we had become more proficient at tyre retreading and had acquired a couple of Sio presses from a company in Bristol called Fixatyre.

John, my brother, was still at this time continuing to run his company of J. O'Connell & Associates. He had taken on a partner in this business who was an old colleague. His name was Brian Hughes, and he and his wife Gloria had left their city life in London and bought a house in Ivybridge. Brian was an easy going and very witty character who had left it later in life to get married. He was a qualified rubber technologist, the same as John, and had the appearance of the late actor Brian Rix. Having moved down and started to build the business he set off to visit some potential customers in South Africa where he was tragically killed in a car crash. Gloria, his wife, came to stay with us in Modbury for a few days and it was a very sad time. John was involved in getting Brian's body brought back to the UK. Most of Brian's money had been stolen after the accident by persons unknown. This episode really brought J. O'Connell & Associates to a point of no return. John was still able to conduct a few machinery deals and also carry out some work for the United Nations. I helped out where I could with the business and May 1974 saw me on a flight to Singapore to photograph some rubber processing machinery that John had bought unseen from a factory there that had shut down. This was my first visit to a commercial Asian city and I found it fascinating. The humidity was pleasant, especially when it rained and my tee shirt got wet. That was fine until I returned to the hotel and the air conditioning hit me. At that time there was still a lot of the old Singapore left and I wandered around the streets and stumbled across Sago Lane. Here there were several funeral parlours, a relic of the old death houses where the terminally ill came to die. That practice halted in 1961 but the detailed preparation for 'customers' to be transported into the next world was very much alive. Besides building a coffin, the parlour employees were busy making small artefacts such as cars, TVs, etc. for the unfortunate candidate to feel at home within their coffin. I often ate out at the street stalls where the food was very good. It seemed that Singapore never slept. It was flat out 24 hours a day and seven days a week and I remember liking the buzz that it gave off. I stayed at the Royal Ramada

Hotel which was quite upmarket, but prices in those day were low, when sterling was a lot more valuable. Next day I took a cab to the now closed factory to photograph the machinery. I had a 400 ASA film in the camera, which was just as well as the interior of the buildings were dark and dirty. Not being a photographer of note I wondered if they would come out OK. A return visit would not have been a good idea as the people on site were not particularly helpful with my first visit. Happily, when the films were developed all was well and John was able to use them in marketing the machinery. My two days in Singapore soon came to an end and I returned to Modbury and retreading.

My relationship with Linda had become decidedly rocky, and as she was now working away as a teacher, our contact became less and less. It was a pity, as we had enjoyed some wild times together, but work for both of us then took priority. A bit of my heart always stayed with her, though.

Now that we had mastered the art of making tyres black and round and they didn't fall to pieces, it was time to start to look for new business. I started to venture further afield and always carried a few sample tyres that I could show, plus some rather amateur sales leaflets. There were a lot of small haulage companies in the area and gradually we managed to pick up more business.

I eventually headed into Exeter looking for more business and came across a large fleet called Renwick's Transport. The transport manager was called Bob Jones and we seemed to hit it off. They were using Michelin tyres at the time which were quite expensive. We only produced one tyre pattern at the time which was a copy of the Michelin XB pattern and very popular among tipper operators. I regularly picked up five to ten tyres a week from there – much to the disgust of the local Michelin rep who used to hurl abuse at me whenever we came into contact.

There was also a large transport fleet based in Plympton near Plymouth called Heavy Transport. They were owned by English China Clay and had about 200 tipper trucks based at this depot alone. They also had a much larger depot in St Austell, Cornwall.

My brother John made the call here and having taken the management out for a rather splendid lunch, as was the custom in those days, they said they would try some of our tyres. At the time they were using tyres from a competitor of ours based in Castle Cary, Somerset called Tyre Renewals. We ended up sharing the business with them for a couple of years. A lot of business in those times resulted in some fairly hefty lunchtime drinking sessions plus some scary drives home afterwards. One such session ended in an employee falling out of the back door of a car travelling over Dartmoor. Apparently, no one realised until the rest stopped to relieve themselves in a layby.

Some tyre presses came onto the market in Bristol from a company called Fix a Tyre. They were SIO presses and were air/hydraulic operated which at the time seemed like space age technology to us. The introduction of more presses into an area with a low ceiling made the working conditions intensely hot in summer. If you weren't covered and you touched a press you immediately got a scorch mark. So with stained black hands and scorch marks up our arms, social life was somewhat limited.

The early seventies provided some challenging times for a company just starting out. We were hit with the miners' strike which resulted in the three-day week. We therefore had to extend our hours to make in three days what we would normally make in five. We would go out selling and collecting tyres when the shutdown was active. There was also a shortage of oil. Our boiler was oil fired and used quite a lot of fuel. Fortunately my sister-in-law's family owned a very large farm and stocked a lot of diesel which they didn't use much of in the winter months. We used this as a fall-back option to keep going. Despite all the setbacks we were making money; mainly because we didn't spend any. We worked nine-hour days and half days on Saturdays. When things started to get busy, I drove the truck during the day and would go back to John and Sally's for tea. I would then pick up another of our workers called Fred Lowry in Modbury and mould tyres until 10 pm when we would rush back to The Ebb Tide pub in Aveton Gifford on our way home for three pints of Guinness.

After a couple of years it was becoming difficult to operate our expanding business out of the 1,000 square feet of floor space that we rented. Adding more machinery into that small space was becoming problematic not only because of the heat but also because of the amount of silicone mould release that we were using and putting out into the non-vented building which was also used for car respraying. Sam, the car spraying guy cursed us constantly because small blisters would appear on his new paintwork. Ted, the cockney caretaker, also hated us with a vengeance as we stored all our bags of buffing dust and scrap tyres outside on the ramp that led into our top floor area. The final straw came for Ted when one day he thought I had set him up. We occupied part of the top floor of the two-storey building. On the ground floor were the service bays for Tally Ho Coaches who owned the building. The new engine oil for the coaches was held in a large 500-gallon tank on the bank outside of our door. The oil was pumped via an air pump from the tank into the building. When a fitter was working on a coach and had drained the engine oil he would grab a nozzle, not dissimilar from a petrol pump nozzle and pull the lever to dispense the oil into the engine. On the day in question I was walking past the tank and heard air escaping. I was standing wondering if there was a fault with the system when around the corner came Ted. I told him that there was an air leak on the pipe going to the tank. He jumped up onto the tank and immediately triumphantly stated that he had spotted the problem; the pipe had become disconnected. Being always prepared, Ted pulled an adjustable spanner from his overalls pocket and reconnected the pipe. The pump immediately started busily pumping. Ted admiringly stood on top of the tank, spanner in hand, when suddenly the side door of the building burst open and a guy emerged covered in oil shouting, 'Who put that bloody pipe on? I'm working on installing a new pipeline!' Ted never forgave me for this incident and made life as difficult as he could for us.

The small Bedford 'coffin truck' was becoming too small for the amount of business that we were generating. It was also very underpowered and with a full load of tyres every hill became a challenge. At this time I had a girlfriend who lived in Richmond and worked at Selfridges. Some Friday evenings I would jump in the Mini

Traveller that I had, and drive up to meet Tricia at Richmond for the weekend. Whilst looking through a truck magazine one day I noticed a Ford D series box van with tail lift for sale in Feltham, not too far from Richmond. I travelled by train to Paddington on Friday and took a look at the truck. It seemed tidy apart from a cut in the front tyre. I said if they changed the tyre we would have a deal and I would pick it up on Sunday and drive it back. I picked the truck up as planned complete with replacement tyre and drove it back to Modbury. It had a six- cylinder engine and so was a lot more powerful than the old Bedford and also looked quite tidy as it had been sprayed in a midnight blue colour. It could also carry a lot more tyres and the tail lift meant we were moving upmarket with our technology. All seemed to be going well with the truck until one of the fitters from Tally Ho coaches was servicing it one day and happened to mention that he didn't know I had a heavy goods vehicle licence, which caused a rather awkward silence. My brother had acquired his HGV licence by 'Grandfather's Rights' claiming he had been driving his in-laws' cauliflower delivery truck. We bought some L plates and booked me in for a driving test. This was made more pressing as a result of a motorist who hit the side of the truck in a narrow road and wanted my insurance details. The day of the test subsequently arrived and I was feeling quite confident as I had been driving the truck almost every day for about four months. I thought I was doing OK until the questions arrived and I answered them as best as I could. What I didn't realise was that there are set questions and set answers that you must give. The one question that sticks in my mind is: "What would you do in the event of brake failure with your truck?" I subsequently found out that the correct answer is: 'Stop; park safely until the fault is rectified' – not shout Geronimo! and leap out of the cab.

I then went for some unofficial driving lessons on a Sunday morning with Ron Facey, the driver trainer from Heavy Transport. He was very good and gave me several tips. One of the examiner's favourite tricks, apparently, was that during the test he would sit well forward in his seat so that you couldn't see the passenger side rear-view mirror mounted on the door. He would then fail you on insufficient use of mirrors. This he did during my test and I asked him if he wouldn't mind sitting back, which together with answering the set questions, to which I now knew the answers to, resulted in a pass.

The bigger truck meant that I could now travel farther as it was faster than the old Bedford. It could also carry a bigger payload. The building of the dual carriageway from Exeter to Plymouth had resulted in a lot of work for us and enabled us to perfect our tyre moulding techniques as a few disasters didn't seem to matter. Provided we gave them another tyre, they were happy. This was a time when truck drivers fitted their own tyres in operations such as this. When the building work of the dual carriageway finished the owners of the trucks parked them all and disappeared.

As we were now beginning to seriously outgrow our capacity and our welcome at Tally Ho coaches, we needed to look for somewhere larger. The problem with being based in Kingsbridge was that it took half an hour to access the Plymouth to Exeter dual carriageway, therefore wasting an hour's driving each trip as most of our business seemed to be developing via this corridor. John went on the hunt for some better premises but nothing seemed to be available except for some extra ground being released by South Hams District Council on the Lee Mill industrial estate near Ivybridge. This estate had been home to a RAF camp during the Second World War and had already been partially developed, but a lot of the site still lay derelict.

We acquired a site of about 30,000 square feet quite near the entrance to the industrial estate. John mortgaged his house and managed to raise enough funds for us to have the site excavated and get a 4,000-square feet building erected.

In the meantime I had also managed to raise a mortgage and bought a three bedroom Wimpey house at 3 Longbrook Road, Ivybridge. I had no idea about living on my own but quickly managed to get a few household appliances on the cheap to set up home. I had a small plastic fridge which stood on the floor and a Belling cooker which sat on top of the fridge. Over a period of time the cooker gradually melted its way into the fridge, but the set-up worked. I also had my own telephone which was a revelation and meant that I could directly contact and hear from people in privacy. It seems strange now, but that gave me a great sense of freedom. I had also at this point become very involved with the Ivybridge Dramatic Society. This led to a somewhat interesting social life which I won't elaborate on here.

    This would have been around 1974. We were still working in Kingsbridge but now had the empty shell of a new building to fit out. The building consisted of two very small offices with a toilet, work toilets and a shower for the factory, a small restroom and a services building for the boiler and compressors. The lighting and domestic plumbing had already been installed as part of the building. This left the heavy electrics and steam pipework to be completed. Neither John nor I were certified for three-phase electrical installation and so we contracted this out. I was fairly well versed in steam installations having studied this as part of my Plant Engineering course. We purchased a small Perkins boiler that ran on diesel oil plus a two-stage piston compressor, and evenings and weekends set about installing the steam and condensate return lines. When everything was ready we said goodbye to Tally Ho Coaches and moved the equipment to Lee Mill. The set-up worked well, although the automatic early morning startup of the boiler didn't always work as well as we hoped but more often than not the presses were up to steam when we started at 8 am each morning. We now had some semblance of a production line, although everything was lifted from one place to another by hand. The pipework and presses had no lagging and with the steam at 150 degrees centigrade the temperatures in the summer months could get very high. Tempers among the guys who were shall I say, of a physical nature, could then become quite strained. At that time I was also fairly ruggedly built and was able to 'mediate' and keep control. We were now making about a hundred tyres a week and I was covering most of Cornwall and Devon collecting and delivering tyres. Tyre building now became a bottleneck. We had to hold so many different sizes of tread rubber (Camelback) that storage and ordering was becoming a problem. We decided to investigate an American machine called an Orbitread. It was manufactured by AMF (American Machines and Foundries) and extruded rubber in a hot flat trip which it wound onto the tyre in a programmed profile. This meant that all we had to do was buy pallets of uncured strip rubber and programme the machine to build profiles set on a punch card. The agent was in Whitstable in Kent and so one day, John, Will Sloman (who was our foreman) and I, set off to look at the machine in action. It seemed to be just what we wanted and so we ordered one. It was on a lease arrangement and so didn't need a lot of money up front. The machine duly arrived and AMF sent an engineer to install it and offer training. He was called Steve, a nice guy who liked a drink! The machine worked very well and speeded up production and also saved us space from storing boxes of rubber compound. It had one weakness though in that every six months rubber compound would worm its way back into the gearbox. This meant that we had to strip the whole machine down and clean all the gears and bearings. Oil which has been mixed with rubber under heat is a rather unpleasant substance to work with and we got filthy during this operation.

We kept going and replaced the buffing machine with a brand new Italmatic 64. It was a very powerful machine that worked to an adjustable template to give the tread profile.

Over the next three to four years we added a 5,000 square feet building and an 8,000 square feet building to the site. In the larger building we installed a 60-inch mixing mill and began to produce our own rubber compounds. We did this under a separate company name called Devon Rubber. The thought was that maybe we could sell rubber compounds to other retreaders. We employed a guy called Tony Barney to run the new venture. Tony was a larger than life character who had studied rubber technology at the same college as my brother. He had apparently been deported from Malaysia and Greece. In Malaysia he had worked as a rubber consultant for the government but when trying to lift some heavy machinery with a hoist attached to the roof only succeeded in pulling the whole building down. He then worked in Greece without a work permit and picked an argument with a policeman when told he was parked illegally. Tony's enthusiasm knew no bounds. On Saturday mornings we used to catch up with machinery maintenance. One morning, Bernard, our part-time electrician, spent about two hours rebuilding a very complicated long cylindrical switch. It had a series of small rollers and springs and had to be carefully put together in sections. We were in the tea room having our morning break when Bernard appeared through the door holding the switch like a baby in his arms. He stated that he had just managed to get all the components in their rightful places and he was now going to screw the whole thing back together. Tony, in his enthusiasm said, "Oh let's have a look," and grabbed the switch which then fell on the floor scattering the rollers, springs, etc. around the tea room.

Tony was also into health and fitness and bought himself a bicycle when he lived in Plymouth. He then acquired a small inflatable dinghy complete with oars and outboard. He somehow managed to attach the whole ensemble onto his bicycle to transport it. One afternoon he transported his rubber boat down to the waterside in Plymouth, assembled and inflated the dinghy; attached the motor, loaded the oars and set off towards the Eddystone lighthouse some 13 miles out to sea. Unfortunately, having got a considerable way offshore, the mooring rope from the front of the boat went under it and caught around the propeller. The result was that the propeller wound the rope around itself and folded the dinghy in half pushing the outboard under the water and thus killing the engine. Tony was left sitting on an inflated ball and had to spend all afternoon and evening paddling himself back to shore.

We had also started to expand out of the south-west and into South Wales where we picked up quite a large amount of work supplying tyres into the Port Talbot steelworks. They used a lot of tyres on trucks that carried slag away from the blast furnaces. The tyres suffered cuts from scrap steel and also fire damage from the hot clinker. We made a cross ply tyre from casings from the Cardiff bus company. By their nature cross ply tyres are very heavy construction and worked well in the application. The tyre depot that supplied the tyres into the steelworks was owned by a nice guy called Tudor Clanfield. He always seemed to get the steelworks contract and paid his bills on time.

Some other business that we acquired was with a company called Key Transport who had a depot in Kingsteignton near Newton Abbot. They were a satellite depot for a London transport company and operated a night trunk transport service. They ran mainly Ford tractor units that were notoriously unreliable but cheap. Based at the Kingsteignton depot was Ronnie Witts the manager and Dougie the mechanic. Dougie was kept busy constantly changing engines and gearboxes on his own while Ronnie operated out of a portacabin on site. Ronnie paid the bills from a cheque book in which each cheque was limited to a maximum of £9. When I delivered the tyres he had to frantically write out a load of cheques to settle the account.

The three buildings that we had on the one site were not now big enough to accommodate our production and so in 1982 we bought an adjoining site just below the present one and built another building which incorporated a large meeting room where we could entertain customers on their visits. This building became the casing and finished tyre store. I was now spending quite a lot of time on the road finding enough casings to keep the factory going. I was driving about a thousand miles a week. We had a sort of depot in Wigan at Eckersley Mill. The building was rented by a guy called Norman Clarry who was a somewhat unusual character. He was a short man with a tweed coat who spoke with a very posh accent and constantly took snuff and blew his nose into a red spotted handkerchief. Norman always hankered after the old days when his family had servants and held bridge parties. He often used to say to my brother and me that his quality of life had declined over the years but "people like YOU! Your lives have improved!" His life had gradually descended into becoming a casing dealer, not that there wasn't money to be made in this occupation. He lived in Plympton but commuted to Wigan each week. He initially started out by selling us casings but he soon saw an opportunity whereby perhaps he could sell our tyres in the North. Norman approached a tyre distribution company called National Tyre Services and we soon established a working relationship with them. At the time, they were owned by Dunlop who had their own retreading works but the retreads that they produced were not of the best quality and NTS found it difficult to pitch the Dunlop truck tyre retread against the retreads manufactured by Michelin. We set up a deal with NTS, that outside of the south-west of England, they would have the exclusive right to sell Bandvulc tyres. This in effect meant that we now had a very large network with the NTS sales team promoting our product. The relationship worked well and expanded *from just distributing in the north of England to also distributing in the Midlands. We would have regular meetings with the NTS and also employed a few of their retired sales guys to help the relationship. This meant that we spent very little money on sales literature and marketing. We could now concentrate on the technical aspect of the business which is where our hearts really lay. NTS changed CEOs from time to time but the relationship continued. We were approached by other tyre distributors to supply them in NTS regions but we stuck to our word to only supply NTS. Once again NTS were changing their CEO, and John and I were invited to head office at Stockport to meet him. He didn't seem as friendly as the previous CEOs. During the meeting, which seemed to be going quite well, he thanked us for the tyres that we'd supplied but said there was going to be a change to their business model. They would no longer be supplying one make of retread, i.e. ours, but that they were a multi-brand company and from now on would be supplying whatever retread the customer specified. This came as a severe shock to John and me as over the past five years we had completely relied upon them to do our sales and marketing. When we left his office and drove back to Ivybridge I don't think either of us said a word. We really didn't know what effect this meeting was going to have on our business. We had completely relied on one customer to take most of our production. When we returned to the factory we constantly watched what happened to our sales orders. We started to approach other distributors in the NTS regions and now offered them the opportunity to stock and distribute Bandvulc tyres. But the question was, would they want to use them?*

Chapter 6

Married Life

My social life became quite active based around the local amateur dramatic group. I performed in quite a few plays such as Boeing Boeing, Two and Two make Sex, and being only in my mid-twenties I usually got the role of playing the young lothario. The group had a busy social side with regular barbecues and parties. We put on some revues in pubs and also at Salcombe Ladies Hockey Club summer barbeque. We set up a stage in the hockey field using a Bandvulc lorry as a changing room with it backed onto a farm trailer that formed the stage. Some of the sketches that we performed were far from being 'politically correct' and would be banned now but we had some great fun and often laughed until we cried doing them.

We had one lady called Janice who joined our motley band. She was married to Tom and came from Cheltenham. She was a keen 'am drammer' and soon fitted in well with the group. One night she brought her younger sister Shela along to a rehearsal. After the rehearsal we all went to the pub as usual, and Janice and Shela were also there. Shela and I got talking and there seemed to be a mutual attraction. Shela was blond, good looking with a relaxed attitude and we seemed to warm to each other. There was one problem, however, and that was that Shela was in a very unhappy marriage. This was around 1975 and there was always a problem with her husband appearing and taking her back to Cheltenham, but eventually she broke free and started working in the laundry at Moorhaven psychiatric hospital which was in Bittaford, a small village about two miles from Ivybridge. She worked hard and became well liked there and then applied to become an EMN (Enrolled Mental Nurse). She got accepted and began her training. She moved into the nurses' home and built a strong circle of friends there. The hospital had a very active social club with a lot of activities. In the time since

1974, I had moved from 3 Longbrook Road to 'Highlands'. Highlands was a large property in the centre of Ivybridge and sat within about two acres of wooded grounds. The main house was divided into three being West, South and East Highlands. West Highlands had come onto the market and lying with the grounds was an old squash court which had been roughly converted into a three-bedroom house. The internal design was built around a central atrium with skylights. There were only windows at either end of the house. John and I put in a successful bid for the property and then divided it out so that he lived in West Highlands and I took up residence in the Squash Court. It was quite a magical house, especially on a summer's morning when the birds would be singing in the trees outside and a warm breeze wafted in through the old wooden windows.

Our Mum died of breast cancer in 1977; it was so sad to see her fading away and then being taken into a hospice where she passed away. Dad said that he wanted to look after her at home but her health had gone beyond what he could cope with. Mum had always been very anti Catholic but when she was in the hospice she took up Catholicism. I asked her why she had changed her mind and she said that she owed it to the nuns who had regularly visited and comforted her. She was buried in Newton Abbot cemetery at Ogwell on the Totnes road just outside of Newton Abbot. I took in our Dad and also took in a guy who worked for us called Ross Swift. He had had a difficult family background and settled in OK until he had some sort of breakdown and left. I had also made friends with two foreign teaching students, and so people were constantly dropping in, and we had some great parties there. The two foreign students were Werner Hoffmann from Forcheim in Germany and Pierre Gueyraud from France. We are still penfriends today and we all got married and had children at about the same time.

Our Dad was still living with me up until about 1978. I was on the road for most of the time and he spent a lot of time on his own. We were fortunate to find him a council bungalow nearby that had emergency cover and other people around him who were in a similar situation. He was very content there on his own and we took him food and also to Mass on Sundays. He had gone to some basket weaving classes and had become quite taken with it. We were supplied with a constant stream of serving trays, flowerpots, etc. and began running out of room to put them all. I think he started to get early signs of some sort of dementia because he would occasionally say that he could see piles of ants. This could sometimes become a source of embarrassment. He had often mentioned his fascination with the ants that he had seen when burning charcoal in the woods at Moretonhampstead during the war. It seems they were very prolific there. One day he had a chest infection and became somewhat unwell and so the carers suggested a temporary stay in a local rest home in Ivybridge. We used to visit him regularly and often found him sitting with the other residents in front of the communal TV. While sitting and chatting with him one day he pointed out that there was something moving around under the TV. He insisted that he could see something and asked me to take a look. While I was on my hands and knees under the TV he said, 'How many ants are there?' I think I counted to ten before getting back up and sitting back down with him.

He also started to get a bit worried about being broken into and asked if I could lend him my 12 bore. I tried to delay giving it to him but he became quite insistent. I relented and took him the gun but he also wanted some cartridges which I also begrudgingly gave him. I warned my brother that when he went to see him to make sure he made himself known before confronting him, especially at night. One day he was quite ill with a chest infection and we called the doctor. We met the doctor on the doorstep and duly took him in to see Dad who was in bed. The doctor pulled back the bed sheets to examine his chest only to see the 12 bore lying across it. The funny thing was, he never mentioned it, just lifted it out of the way and carried on with the examination.

In 1981 Shela and I had been together on and off for about seven years. It seemed that we were coming back together more and more often. Shela was keen to start a family and I had to admit to myself that I very much loved her and that our future would be together. As Shela was divorced and I was a Roman Catholic a church wedding was out of the question and so we lived together until Shela fell pregnant and then we decided it was time to make our relationship formal and we were married in Plymouth Registry Office on July 25th 1981.

For our honeymoon, Shela and I went to Los Angeles. We were a little worried about the trip as Shela was now pregnant with Ryan, but a check at the doctors confirmed that all would be well. Shela's friend Liz had shared a house in Ivybridge with a guy called Keith who had now moved to work for Manpower in LA. We still had little money between us, and Keith had offered to accommodate us on our trip for which we were very grateful. Keith shared a flat with a very laidback guy called George and we had a great first week with them, meeting their friends and going to numerous parties and barbeques. We planned our second week in Las Vegas and stayed at The Grand Hotel. We travelled there by Concorde. Not the aircraft but a hire car made by Chrysler. I was nicknamed Captain Trubshaw by Keith and his friends. At that time Las Vegas was in the last years of being run by the Mafia and rooms, food and drink were very cheap. So long as you didn't gamble you could enjoy a cheap luxury holiday and see some really excellent shows. While we were there we met up with a UK casing dealer from London called Bob Taylor that we did business with. Bob and his wife were regular visitors to Las Vegas and took us out to one of their favourite restaurants called Bob Taylors Ranch House. The Ranch House is still in existence. The food was American size portions and I remember having the lamb chops which were of course much bigger than English lamb chops. Before leaving we took a drive to the Grand Canyon and were overawed by the size of it. It is very unusual in that all the ground around is completely flat and then this enormous chasm appears. We then drove back to LA and stayed once again with Keith and George. We found the Californian work ethic somewhat different to ours; although on the outside it seemed vary laid back, this disguised a need to be a committed company person. Early morning discussions over coffee and doughnuts plus Saturday company barbeques were really mandatory events if you wished to gain credit and move further up the corporate ladder.

Returning to LA led to more parties and beach barbeques and then back to the UK. Shela was now about three months pregnant and beginning to develop a 'bump'. We started to attend antenatal classes

Wedding July 1981

where it was explained what we could expect leading up to the baby's birth. We also made a tour of the Special Care Baby Unit (SCBU) at Freedom Fields hospital. The visit was interesting but to be honest, I didn't pay a lot of attention as I thought all would be well with our birth, but as time went on that assumption would prove to be ill founded.

On 1st December 1981 Shela and I had arranged for a guy that we were doing some machinery dealing with to stay with us overnight. When I brought him home that evening Shela was preparing dinner when she suddenly said that she had a terrible backache and needed to lie down. Our guest seemed happy to take over the preparation of the dinner while I helped Shela to the bedroom and called the doctor. The doctor arrived quite promptly and announced that Shela was in labour and needed to go to Freedom Fields maternity hospital immediately. She already had a bag packed and so we left our guest to finish preparing his own meal and set off quickly to the hospital. On arrival Shela was immediately found a bed and wired up to monitor her and the baby's condition. We were both somewhat overawed by the procedure having suddenly been thrust into a medical drama and not knowing what the outcome might be. At around midnight Shela's contractions started to seriously kick in. I think we were both wondering the same thing: would the baby survive being born six weeks early? The contractions continued and gradually got worse until at 2 am Ryan was born. He weighed just over four pounds and looked extremely fragile. I was overwhelmed at his arrival and admit that I was in tears, especially to see that he was alive and the midwives assured us that he would be fine. He was rushed away and put into an incubator to keep him warm. Being premature he was very sleepy and never cried. As he wasn't strong enough to breastfeed, Shela had to express her milk into bottles, put her name on them and then store them in a large refrigerator with all the other mothers' milk bottles on the ward. Ryan was then fed every four hours via a syringe and tube which went through his nose and into his stomach. Shela stayed with him at the hospital and I went home to get some sleep and prepared to settle into the new role of being a parent. I went to visit the next day and all seemed to be OK but of course Shela was very tired and somewhat sore having had some stitches as a result of Ryan's appearance. That second evening John and I had a customer outing which had been planned for some time. It was to see Pyjama Tops, a raunchy show of the time, at the Princess Theatre, Torquay. I was still feeling somewhat tired and confused by what had happened in the last 48 hours but after the show John bought a bottle of champagne and we raised a toast to Ryan and Shela.

After a couple of days Shela returned home and commuted to and from the hospital during the day with me taking her down in the evenings. The weather always seemed to be dark and cold and week after week we continued the daily pilgrimage until on New Year's Day they said that Ryan had reached a weight that we could bring him home. The day that we were taking him was very wet, and one of the nurses quipped, "Take them home in the rain and they will be back in again." She was however correct! He was always a very quiet baby and it was sometimes worrying that we heard nothing from him, although he was now able to take milk from the breast and also a bottle.

We were still living in the Squash Court at the time. Access to the property was not the easiest with a lot of stone steps leading down to the front door. We decided that we should start to look for a newer property. Meanwhile Shela became pregnant again and in February 1982 we decided to have a winter break in Tenerife. Ryan was just able to stand at this time and Shela was around three months pregnant and so we set off with all the necessary baby things to stay at a resort in Santa de la Cruz. It was a nice resort although the electrics were a bit dodgy and we kept Ryan's metal cot well away from anything with a wire protruding. On the day we were returning, Ryan was very poorly with a stomach upset and when we got home the doctor booked him straight into Freedom Fields hospital. We were once again into regular hospital visits with Ryan being restricted to small amounts of liquid plus his medication. He gradually pulled through and the doctor, who came from Northern Ireland, said that we could now take him home and give him 'some salads'. Shela and I looked at each other, but the nurse standing by picked up on our puzzled expressions. "He means solids," she whispered!

Summer was coming and we had found a house at 17 Wood Park, Stowford Park, opposite the Ivybridge community college. The house was newly finished and was part of the Stowford Park development by Connoly Homes. We sold the Old Squash Court and paid £58,000 for the new house and moved in around May 1983. It was a very good house with four bedrooms and a large garden with a southerly view down over the valley. It had a double garage with two extra parking spaces in front. The outside road area was extremely muddy from the constant flow of construction traffic but we settled in and the neighbours were very friendly and of similar ages to ourselves, with families. I did have some problems getting the electricity supply switched from Connoly Homes to ourselves. The person at SWEB kept insisting that it was already in our name, i.e. Mr Connoly, and could not seem to understand that Connoly and O'Connell are two different names.

We had very little money as the mortgage was now quite high plus we needed new furniture for the house and Shela started to take driving lessons as a school run would soon be looming. When Shela passed her test I bought a second-hand Austin Allegro for her but it was an awful car and as soon as I had some more money we acquired a Mini Traveller. On 18th August 1983 our daughter Samantha was born. Compared to Ryan's birth it was a much more casual affair. On the morning in question, Shela said that she had started to feel contractions and that the baby would soon be on its way. We made provision for a neighbour to look after Ryan for the day and Shela came to work with me and sat in the office. We had notified the maternity ward of the situation and when the requisite speed of contractions arrived we set off for the hospital and Samantha was born without any complications and within a couple of hours of our arrival. Unlike Ryan, she made us very aware of her presence and was, for the want of a better phrase, a constantly noisy baby.

We had enough money to afford one decent holiday per year and decided that after Ryan's illness when we had gone to Tenerife we needed to stay nearer to home. There was a ferry service from Weymouth to Guernsey and so we rented a cottage on the island and headed off. Unfortunately the ferry operators went on strike soon after we had boarded with our car and the afternoon drifted into evening before we set sail only to arrive into St Peter Port in the dead of night. We had never been to Guernsey before and so we drove off into the darkness with no idea where we were headed. Fortunately Guernsey is not so big and we eventually found our accommodation. We had brought along a girl named Edwina to help out and babysit so that Shela and I would have some time to visit a restaurant or two during our time there. Whilst touring the island we visited the museum and were greeted by a somewhat ancient lady sitting behind a desk. She was very short and only her eyes appeared above the top of the desk. As we paid our entrance fee she enquired as to where we were staying. When I said that we were renting a cottage her eyes lit up and she asked how much we were paying. Innocently I replied that it depended whether it was high season or low season as there were different prices. "Well what about the high season price, then?" she enquired. I could now see where this was going and so I answered, "Well they charge more if a TV is supplied." I then added that it also depended whether you wanted the electricity included in the rent or paid for separately. So quick as a flash the old lady retorted, "OK, high season, including the TV and electricity." By this time a queue was beginning to form behind us and we started to move on to the sound of, "Well, how much?"

Whilst on the island we noticed the St Pierre Park Hotel which seemed very inviting and had a very nice restaurant called the Victor Hugo after the famous writer of Les Misérables who took up residence on the island having been exiled from France for saying that Napoleon III was a very naughty boy. The next year we flew from Plymouth to Guernsey and stayed at the St Pierre Park. It was a very comfortable hotel and was very accommodating for the children. We returned here for the next two or three years until the children were big enough to undertake longer journeys.

We had now settled in to becoming a suburban couple and by 1986 we had set our life up quite well. The children were healthy and starting to attend school or preschool and we were now venturing to Menorca for our annual holiday. We could fly there from Exeter and the island was very pleasant and not so developed as its sister island Majorca. Over the years as the children got bigger we ventured further afield to DisneyLand in Florida and Canada which was one of our favourite trips.

Chapter 7
Flying

There came a point in my life when I decided I needed to confront my fear of flying by becoming a pilot. The year was 1980, and Shela and I set off to Exeter Flying Club one Saturday afternoon for a trial lesson. The club was based in a large single storey World War Two type building adjacent to the airfield. There was a bar and coffee/tea making facilities and although there was a professional air about the place, the people there seemed friendly. We met our instructor who was called Rufus, who gave Shela and me a basic rundown on how an aircraft flies, which has always remained a mystery to me. Rufus took me up first for the trial lesson in a Cessna 150 two-seater. The Cessna 150 is a high wing aircraft and despite all the knobs and buttons is a pretty simple design. It seemed very cramped in the cockpit and the 150 flies in a rather peculiar nose high attitude which means that the view ahead is mainly of the propeller and the sky. I can't say that I really enjoyed that first lesson. Rufus struck me as a somewhat aloof ex RAF character and I was still racked with my fear of flying. I did fly the aircraft for part of the time but didn't seem to yet grasp the fundamentals. We landed back at the airport and Shela took her turn. It seemed that Rufus and Shela didn't gel and she never took another lesson. I was determined to continue and so joined the club and signed up for more lessons. I booked another lesson with Rufus when he introduced me to stalling the aircraft. I was still somewhat apprehensive but having carried out a couple of stalls which required reducing the power and pulling the stick gradually back until the aircraft nose suddenly dropped I started to feel somewhat in control. What Rufus did next, though, put me firmly back to square one. As I was approaching the stall Rufus suddenly kicked in a boot full of left rudder and the aircraft went into a spin. At that time I had no idea what a spin was and all I could see was fields, sky and sea whizzing past the windscreen. Rufus then pulled the aircraft out of the spin and calmly said, "That was a spin, which can develop from a stall."

I then changed instructors to a guy called Keith Chambers. Keith had flown Liberators at the end of the Second World War and was a very relaxed pilot. I always felt that if the wings were to fall off Keith would have some 'cunning plan' that would save the day. I did a few more stalls and spins with Keith but he always explained beforehand what was going to happen and how to recover the aircraft. Next we went on to 'straight and level' flight which is not so easy as it sounds. To get the aircraft perfectly trimmed so that it flies without gaining or losing height is an acquired knack that took me a few lessons to grasp. We then did a lot of 'circuit bashing', and appreciating the different landing approaches and configurations. On a final approach after having logged eight hours flying I heard Keith notifying the controller that we would be coming to a stop on the runway, which after landing we duly did. Keith then started to get out of the aircraft telling me to do my first solo. He also added that if I wasn't happy with my final approach to go around and try again but that I only had fuel for two hours after which I would have to land. I called up the tower who informed me that I was clear for take-off and so I opened the throttle and off I went. The aircraft became airborne much quicker with just me and so up I went to 600 feet, turned onto my crosswind leg and got up to the circuit height of 800 feet and then turned down wind flying parallel to runway 26 on which I was due to land. I now had a little time to reflect on my situation and how alone I suddenly felt, but it was time to get busy again and call up: 'Downwind to land for 26', and receive clearance. Turn base leg, throttle back to 1700, wait for the speed to reduce to within the white arc, lower 20 degrees of flap and turn onto final approach. 'Keep the piano keys just on top of the nose', as Keith had repeatedly told me, reduce the speed to around 60 knots and once over the runway slowly reduce the power whilst pulling the stick back so as not to let the nose drop. There was a reassuring slight squeak of the main wheels as they touched the runway followed by the nose wheel also kissing the tarmac. On returning to the club there was a small celebration for me completing my first solo. The date was 16th February 1980.

Flying then became more intense, having to tackle cross country jaunts. This started with what was called a 'triangle'. You flew a cross country triangular route. This was Exeter to Bridgwater, south to Sidmouth, and then west back to Exeter; about a one-hour round trip. We had to prepare a route plan with waypoints and times which we marked off on route. This triangle route was quite easy to cheat as after take-off all you had to do was follow the M5 to Bridgwater then turn south and hopefully end up over Sidmouth but if you didn't, just turn right when you got to the sea and eventually the Exe estuary would appear with the airfield at the head of it. The Cessna 150 and 152 were not my favourite aircraft to fly because of the high nose attitude. It was virtually impossible to see anything ahead unless you were in a descent. The seat catches were also very fiddly and temperamental. One of my solo cross country flights I remember was over Axminster. I hit some really bad turbulence and the seat rail locks became loose and I shot backwards away from the controls. My sudden backward movement upset the trim of the aircraft and it suddenly went nose up. I couldn't reach the controls to correct this and so had to dig my nails into the window ledge in order to try to edge myself forward. This resulted in a couple of unscheduled aerobatics while I slowly shuffled myself forward to get back at the controls.

There then followed cross country flights, landing at other airfields. The favourites that fitted the bill were Bristol, Compton Abbas and Swansea. Compton Abbas was on a hill in Dorset and was a grass runway. Not the easiest location to find, particularly when the weather is hazy and you are map reading trying to find a grass field among several other grass fields. Bristol was what is known as a control zone. This means that entry to it is very strictly controlled and you have to get permission to enter the zone at a specific point, not just appear over the horizon and bumble around until you find a runway you like the look of. Swansea was quite a large old airport with a long runway and sits out on the Gower Peninsula. It seemed to be mainly used for pleasure flying. Getting there, though, required flying through the air space for Cardiff airport which was also a control zone. The secret to getting through a control efficiently was to appear to the controller that you knew what you were doing. I used to scribble down my 'banter' before I got to the zone so that I could rattle it off in a professional manner in the hope of being accepted as 'one of the chaps'. On your final cross country, which is your qualifying one, you have to take a score sheet with you and pass it to the tower on landing. My qualifying cross country was supposed to be Exeter-Compton Abbas-Bristol. I sat and carefully planned the route and waypoints and just before I was due to leave my instructor announced that Compton Abbas was fogged in and I would have to go to Bristol and Swansea instead. I sat down to replan my route only to be told that there was no time for that as it was getting late and I would have to work it out enroute. I had done a few trips to Bristol and managed to rummage out one of my old flight plans which held good for the leg. On landing I duly presented myself to the tower with my score sheet which was whisked away and pondered over. I was pleased to receive it back with 'good' written in all the boxes. Next off to Swansea and a hop across the Bristol Channel and into Cardiff's airspace. The visibility was quite good and my banter got me through with no problems. I landed at Swansea and once again presented myself to the tower with my marking sheet. The controller said, "What am I meant to do with this?" I said that he had to write good in each of the boxes and give it back to me which he promptly did. I took off but suddenly had an uneasy feeling that I was heading out to sea as all I saw was water on each side of the aircraft. I checked my heading and also rechecked my Direction Indicator, as these can suddenly wander off course for no apparent reason. Everything seemed to tie up and so I kept going. Only when I lowered the nose out of the climb did I see what was happening. I was on course and flying over Swansea Bay. The Cessna nose high altitude during the climb had caused me some confusion but I then settled down to the hour-long flight back to Exeter. Cardiff let me through with no problems and then it was just across the Bristol Channel to Minehead, find a couple of reservoirs to check my route and Exeter and the airport eventually hove into view. After landing I proudly presented my marking sheet to my instructor and collapsed into a chair with a coffee. I had been three hours in the air with three landings and take offs on a route that I had hurriedly put together. I slept really well that night, comfortable with my achievement.

It was now time to get in shape for my test – lots of general flying revision plus practice forced landings, stalls and advance turns. Advance turns are where you imagine having to avoid another flying object and so you steeply bank the aircraft but maintain control. The trick is to keep the nose on the horizon while increasing the bank of the aircraft until it decides it's had enough and wants to become a brick.

My flying test was on 30th November 1980. The CFI took me up and duly put me through my paces. A forced landing practice can be a bit tricky. The CFI suddenly cuts the power and you immediately have to retrim the aircraft for best glide and run through your checks as to why the engine might have died. Having decided that it is definitely dead to the world, it is time to decide where you might like to land and which way the wind is blowing. Hopefully someone will have a bonfire lit to quickly determine this. The CFI will then ask you which field you intend to land in. There is usually a field with a lot of sheep, which gives you your first marker. Cows aren't much good as they are rather dark in colour and not so numerous. The secret then is to say, "The one next to the sheep." This gives you a few more seconds to work out which of the four fields surrounding the sheep is your best bet. He will then come back with, "Which field next to the sheep?" by which time you will have discovered a long flat field heading into wind, and hopefully next to the sheep to make it sound as though you have it all carefully planned. Next, you have to pick your 1,000 feet spot near the field. This is your first port of call before turning finals onto the field. If you've got it right, after turning onto your final approach the near hedge should be sitting on your nose. If it appears a long way away you can only sit and hope that you have enough glide to get to the field. There is one trick you can pull in this situation and that is to tell the examiner you are just going to give the engine a quick blast to keep it warm for the climb out. If the intended hedge is starting to disappear under the nose it is time to start banging down some flaps to slow everything down and get the nose once again where you want it. Fortunately the Cessna 150 has a wide range of flaps and if you have something like a 20-knot headwind, with full flaps it will come down like a helicopter. By the time you have reached 500 feet and the sheep in the adjoining field have gone into panic mode the instructor will tell you to 'climb away'. Having done a bit of straight and level flying plus a few stalls it's time to head back to the field to perform a selection of unknown landings. Probably starting with a standard rejoin. This means joining overhead at 2,000 feet and letting down into the inactive part of the circuit before joining crosswind and then into the pattern. You may then have to perform perhaps a flapless landing, maybe a bad weather circuit and a few other stunts that the examiner may dream up. I was lucky to pass my General Flying Test on my first attempt. I could now take passengers and my first trip was with Shela when we flew down to Dartmouth and back on 28th December 1980.

Having completed my training I now felt rather on my own. There had been a group of us going through the Student Pilot Training which required meeting up for lectures on Sunday mornings to learn about Engines and Airframes, Navigation and Air Law. We used to compare notes about our various mishaps and an air of camaraderie had developed but that was now over and so, what to do next? We had one Cessna 150 which was an Aerobat, which meant that it was cleared for aerobatics and so I decided to give that a go. My first aerobatic lesson was on 14th February 1980 with Keith who had been my main instructor for my GFT. It was a very cold overcast morning, but Keith said we were good to go. There was cloud cover at about 2,000 feet but Keith said it was relatively thin and we could climb through it, which we did. I didn't know how I would react and expected aerobatics to be quite a violent experience but in the Cessna it turned out to be quite banal. A loop was relatively straightforward, almost literally, put the aircraft into a shallow dive and when it reaches 120 knots, full power and pull the stick back as far as it will go. Check through the skylight as we go over that the wings are parallel to the horizon and back into a dive, reducing the power and hopefully feeling a slight bump as we hit our own slipstream. What seemed odd to me was it seemed as though the aircraft had remained stationary and the world had just rolled past the windscreen. We did a few more loops and barrel roles and Keith seemed happy that I was OK and could now have a go in my own time. With my newfound skill I took Shela up for a spot of aerobatics and continued to do a few joy rides that included aerobatics for a couple of years.

I then signed up for my night flying training. Night flying is much different to day flying. Roads and towns are easily identifiable but line features such as railways and rivers are now lost from view. When we were training for our private pilot's licence we had to do a lot of simulated engine failure and forced landing training. I noticed this was missing from night flying and asked the instructor what the procedure was for engine failure during night flying, only to be told that there isn't one. He suggested, "Head for a dark area and turn on your landing light, if you don't like what you see, turn it off again." Very helpful! The one tricky thing about night flying is that clouds are invisible and it is quite easy to fly into cloud without knowing that it is there.

Next came my training for Flying IMC (Instrument Meteorological Conditions). This qualification enables a pilot to fly outside of controlled airspace in pretty much zero visibility. Flying now became a very intense operation. Flying whilst constantly scanning the instruments plus navigating and communicating puts a lot of strain on a pilot new to this type of flying. Your senses are telling you one thing but the instruments are telling you something different and it is a constant fight to disbelieve your senses and believe what the instruments are telling you. I did eventually master it, but instrument flying is something that you have to do often before you can really relax into it. The day of my test arrived and Ted King the CFI (Chief Flying Instructor|) explained to me before we went out to the aircraft, a route that he wanted me to fly. It was fairly straightforward, west to Ivybridge and then back up to Crediton and return to the airfield for an instrument approach. I planned the route and noted all the navigation and radio frequencies that I would need. When we taxied out and completed the pre-flight checks, I started to put the hood on as I had done for all my IMC lessons, but Ted said, "No need to bother with that, old boy." I thought, "Wow!" This is going to be easy!" But that thought would very quickly be dispelled. It was a thundery day with a lot of towering cumulus cloud. Cumulus cloud can give rise to quite severe turbulence when you least expect it. Looking out of the windscreen your eyes are straining to find a horizon but of course

Ryan and I after a flight

there isn't one, only a lot of different shapes and angles of the cloud. No matter how tempting it is to look outside, you must keep fixed on the instruments. After flying a few different headings and altitudes Ted instructed me to fly back to the airfield. I tuned in the direction finder to 337 which was the airfield beacon and off we set. I was busy working out an ETA and approach when I noticed that the direction needle seemed to be now pointing in a different direction. On closer examination I discovered that Ted had switched it to Radio 4 so that he could hear the cricket results. I quietly switched it back again and we made our approach to the airfield with Ted throwing in a couple of 'unusual attitudes' to destabilise my approach and to see if I could recover the aircraft from them, which I did. On landing, Ted stated that I was OK to fly IMC and signed my log book accordingly. Although I never really did much IMC flying after that, it gave me the confidence to know that if I was caught out by bad weather I stood a chance of finding my way home.

Chapter 8

Scotland

Our sales through NTS did seem to hold up but of course we did not know who the end customers were. Although now able to supply any tyre distributor in the UK we realised how vulnerable our business was. Although sales stayed positive, we were very much exposed to constant price competition from other retread manufacturers. This meant we had a very unstable business model and made future investment planning difficult. We needed to somehow break away from being 'just another retread' supplier. The loss of the NTS exclusive business also resulted in the demise of our snuff-taking agent, Norman. He decided he wanted out and promptly disappeared leaving some question marks as to how he had operated his business. We took over the warehouse from him and the distribution for the north of England.

Scotland was a complete unknown territory to us and it was a surprise to be contacted by the MD of NTS Scotland to invite us to set up an exclusive deal with them as there was no retreader of any size able to cover the whole area. They had some spare room in their depot in Stirling and we came to an arrangement to take on one of their ex-employees to run the depot and carry out the distribution. The orders would be phoned direct to our Wigan depot. We had a spare 7.5 tonne Mercedes box van and so one July Sunday morning with a full load of tyres I set off for Stirling. I reached the depot by late afternoon and checked into the hotel that we had booked. I planned to stay for the week and tour around Scotland with our new employee.

Next morning I arrived at the depot and met our new man. He seemed able enough and went under the name of Cash. He explained that he played guitar and sang country songs in the pubs at night and specialised in Johnny Cash songs. I got the impression that he probably liked a drink; but then so do 99 per cent of the Scottish population. We already had a list of stock orders to deliver and so set off up the west coast. The west coast is very beautiful in July and the scenery was quite breathtaking. We covered Oban and Fort William and returned to the depot. It became obvious that to cover the north of Scotland we would need to make it a two-day trip and stop off somewhere enroute. The next day we set off with a full load of tyres and headed towards Inverness carrying out a few extra deliveries on route. As we neared Inverness we needed to find somewhere to spend the night. We tried some local accommodation directories without much success but did eventually find a bed and breakfast on a farm. The farm was quite isolated and the owner was a famous sheepdog trainer. We parked the truck and knocked on the door. We were shown to our respective rooms; we then asked what time the evening meal would be. We were told that they didn't do food in the evenings but we could walk to the local village and could probably find something to eat there. Having had a wash and brush up we set off to walk to the local village. There didn't seem to be a restaurant or a pub in the village and so we asked one of the locals where we would find the nearest pub. He pointed to a building that looked like a village hall and said that was the local pub. It was quite an austere building with just four block walls and a corrugated roof. We opened the door and went in. The bar area was packed with local people, a thick cloud of smoke hung in the air. When we entered a silence immediately fell on the congregation. It was obvious that they didn't have many strangers visiting. We ordered a couple of beers and sat at a table and ordered some food, all the time inhaling thick clouds of tobacco smoke that seemed to be in different density layers across the room. The conversation once again resumed and we were contemptuously ignored.

Next day we set off and continued around the north of Scotland to Elgin and then on to Fraserburgh. Now, bearing in mind it was a bright sunny July afternoon, Fraserburgh looked to me like some penal colony. The walls along the road were all made of grey granite as were most of the houses. There didn't appear to be any trees and the ones that I did see all leaned at 45 degrees. This seemed to also apply to the people as the wind off the North Sea is particularly unforgiving.

Fishing provided the main income and large fish processing buildings were scattered along the shoreline complete with a plethora of seagulls and the resultant noise and smell that they and the factories produced. I was full of admiration for the people who were happy to live in such a hostile environment. As the week went on I could see that there was good business to be had here and Cash, our new employee, seemed to speak the lingo and was already known to several of the depot managers from his previous employment with NTS. I continued to the end of the week having visited almost all of the depots and flew back down to Plymouth on Friday. Sales continued to grow steadily in Scotland and we were becoming a serious business enterprise.

One of our first exhibiton stands

One of our later exhibition stands

Chapter 9

Big Business

*I*n this chapter I will endeavour to explain how we grew the business from being just a producer of retread truck tyre into a tyre management company.

As I have mentioned in a previous chapter, our sales were predominantly through tyre distributors. This meant that we really had very little control over our sales. We needed to 'court' every tyre depot plus keeping the higher management on our side and also ensuring that we made a high quality product which in turn made them a good profit and hopefully some money for ourselves.

There were two ways that retreads were supplied to distributors. They could either send their own tyres back to us for retreading (C.O.C - customers own casing) or we would supply the tyre and the casing (stock retread). Worn out truck tyres (casings) commanded a high price in the marketplace if they were a quality brand and in good condition. For example a Michelin 385/65R22.5 could be worth up to £50. There were a lot of casing dealers throughout the UK and Europe. Most of the smaller dealers dealt in cash and so I would often set off with a bundle of notes in my pocket in the truck when on a casing buying expedition. The larger casing dealers bought in their casings for cash but when we would probably buy 500 at a time they were then invoiced. The casing dealing world was full of characters. There was one in Manchester who was also a male model and another one whose brother helped him out when he wasn't appearing as an extra in some TV drama. The Manchester guy had a building in the centre of a very large trading estate. Outside of the building was an area of open ground. Each morning when he arrived there would be small piles of tyres assembled on the open ground with different marks on them. He would then make a note of each pile in his notebook and stack them in his warehouse and that was his work for the day. He would then swan off in his 7 series BMW and spend the day visiting and paying off his mates who had dropped off the casings, if he wasn't modelling. Another one was on the London ring road and kept all his casings in the cellar of a house that he owned. We used to pull the tyres out of the cellar and I would inspect them on the pavement beside a bus stop. When the pavement and bus stop were full of tyres we would call in the artic and load it whilst trying to avoid blocking the bus stop. He was a particularly mean Scotsman called Alec. One day I was in South London buying casings, and when I had finished there I went off around the North Circular to visit Alec. He had a full load of casings and so I arranged an artic to arrive later that afternoon. When I got there I was starving, having been on the road since 5 am. I asked Alec if there was a sandwich shop nearby. He said, "There is nae a sandwich round here but there is a bread shop round the corner." I asked him if he could send his assistant to get me a bread roll. He called to Arthur who must have been about 80 years old and said that Arthur would get me a roll, but he would need some money. Now, bearing in mind that I was about to spend a few thousand pounds with Alec he told me to give Arthur fifty pence for the roll. Arthur duly returned with one dry bread roll. Alec then said he could give me some cheese to go with my roll. He took me into his office and opened the fridge door to expose half a bottle of milk and a piece of dried up cheese about the size of my finger. I thought he was going to give me the whole piece of cheese, but no! He went to a small workbench and took a Stanley knife and proceeded to scrape a few shards of cheese onto the roll. He told me that he used to take his girlfriend and stay at the very best hotels but always took his camping stove to prepare meals in his room.

One particular casing buying visit really stuck in my mind. I kept getting phone calls from a casing dealer in Cambridge telling me he always had plenty of casings of the type that we needed. I eventually agreed to go and take a look. I took Nick with me who was our trainee casing buyer and after a five-hour journey checked into a hotel for an early start the next day. The next morning arrived and Nick and I duly turned up at said warehouse to be greeted by a short, ginger-haired man who was the owner that I had spoken to on the phone. After a pleasant enough conversation Nick and I got our overalls and aprons on and the owner, whom I shall call Rob, wheeled out the first casing. I looked at it and saw a big gash in the shoulder of the tyre exposing the wire. I said that it wasn't the quality that we were looking for and we only took first grade casings. Rob then said that that was his first grade, and I should take it. There then followed a bit of a stand-off and I said that as it was the first casing he could throw it in for a fiver. He then went a sort of funny purple colour and said, "Oh I get the idea; offering fancy prices but when you get here it's a different story." There was a small transistor radio playing on a shelf just inside the warehouse door and he walked over to it and threw it against the wall and then said something along the lines of "people like you make me sick." He then stormed off into his office and slammed the door. Nick and I waited for him to come out but he didn't reappear. We had only been on site for about 20 minutes and started to wonder what we could do with the rest of the day. Just then a car rolled up beside us and a guy got out, introduced himself as the manager, and asked us how we were getting on with the inspection. We explained what had happened and that Rob had disappeared into his office and wouldn't come out. The manager said that they had another yard down the road and he had a load that had just come in from Europe and felt there could be some casings there that would fit our grade. It turned out that Nick and I were able to get a load together, but we never returned there. As the factory grew we were travelling to and bringing casings from several countries – Holland, Germany, France, Denmark, Norway and even Japan.

By the end of the 1980s we had started to get really busy. The economy was doing well and we were working in very cramped conditions and still selling a lot of tyres through NTS and of course now other distributors. All of our production had to be moved by hand which meant we had to employ a certain type of employee. Our production was becoming inefficient and so we applied for a government grant to develop a new purpose-built site. We also applied to the local council to purchase a piece of land owned by them, adjoining our present factory. The council told us that we would have to apply for and obtain planning permission before they would sell it to us. We applied for planning and paid the required fee. One day someone dropped by the office and said, "I see you have started work on your new site." We looked and sure enough there was a group of diggers working on digging out the site. We contacted the council who told us that they had sold the site to a developer. We asked if the developer had applied for planning permission and were told that he didn't need it as they had worked on several projects with them and knew what he would build. We then asked for our planning fee to be returned which they refused and we had to apply to the Ombudsman in order to get it returned. We then asked the council for another site on the other side of the industrial estate which they had now started to develop. We were told there was nowhere available for us.

A piece of private ground then came up for sale in Lee Mill village and was right beside the main A38 trunk road to Plymouth. This piece of ground already had planning permission for outside storage. It was probably about an acre in size and situated between the slip road into the village and the main A38 and very visible from both roads. The council heard that we had bought the piece of ground and an official enquired as to what we intended to do with it. "Store casings on it," was our reply. The council were far from happy with this proposal but there was little they could do as planning had already been granted. The idea of having an acre of old tyres stored in a sleepy village next to the dual carriageway didn't seem to appeal to them. They then made a miraculous discovery that actually there may be a site we could purchase on the industrial estate so long as we promised not to store tyres on our newly acquired site.

A site was purchased and we built a 20,000 square foot building for casing storage and buffing. This situation was not ideal as we had to shuttle the buffed tyres in a truck to the old factory for building and moulding. We had also rented some farm buildings about two miles away as temporary casing storage. One day a very angry man appeared at the farm demanding to know where his pile of cow dung was. "Probably where you left it," was our reply, but that just seemed to make him even more angry. "There was two thousand pounds worth of dung in that heap and it's been stolen." We said that he should see the landlord but he was welcome to search the building. He stormed off to see the landlord and we heard no more.

Further investment was required to try to get all production under one roof. We applied for a government grant to build a 40,000 square foot building linked by a tunnel to the buffing building. The grant for £1.5 million of match funding was to be guaranteed by our bank. This put our small town bank manager into somewhat of a tizzy for fear that we might just turn up one day and withdraw one and a half million and disappear. When it was completed it was a wonderful building, but upon finishing there was a problem. When we started the build, interest rates were eight per cent and looked as though they would fall, but during the time we spent constructing the new building, interest rates rose to 15 per cent and there was a recession which meant we were selling fewer tyres than we were before we had moved. We were now paying in the region of £4,000 a week interest. We needed a product that we could corner the market with and steal a march on our competitors to survive; and this came from an unlikely part of the industry.

The waste trucks that collect your household rubbish were notorious for damaging tyres. Drivers would rub them along the side of the pavement until the steel cords showed through the sidewall and they would also drive over an assortment of debris when they tipped their load at waste sites. The industry demanded cheaper and cheaper tyres because of the high damage rate. Besides the damage inflicted on the tyre during its use, a lot of tyres failed because of the inferior quality of the tyre casing and rubber products being used in order to meet a price. We decided that perhaps there was another way to tackle this problem. We took a completely bald tyre to our stand at a waste exhibition which was held annually on the green in Torbay, Devon. We covered the tyre in question marks and asked waste truck operators what were the main problems they found with their tyres and how would they design a tyre for their use. We gained a whole load of comments but there were some common themes that came out of our survey. Sidewall damage was one of the main ones where scuffing along the kerb wore the sidewall away even though the tread might only be half worn. This caused a further problem because the outside tyre became scrap. It was now necessary to fit two replacement tyres because fitting one new one beside one that was 50 per cent worn was not good practice, as the tyre with the most tread could become overloaded. The trucks constantly crashing the tyre against the kerb also tended to break off any lugs in the shoulder area of the tyres. We had enough information to design our first 'Wastemaster' tyre. We designed a tyre with a continuous solid shoulder for the kerb side but also added a thick kerbing band. Under this band we placed a thin layer of red rubber. The purpose of this red rubber was to form an alert for the operator that the sidewall was worn down to the original tyre and the two twin tyres could now be swapped around. No damaged tyres and no tyre fitter was required. The operator could easily swap the wheels around in his workshop. The tyre did have castellated lugs on its other edge for off road traction and we developed a really tough all-natural rubber compound to help combat the puncture problem. We put the tyre into production in a limited way and tested it with a selection of local authorities. The tyre proved a great success and we were able to charge twice the price that we had been selling tyres at previously to the waste industry. The main thing to do with a niche product is to capture the market before your competitors have a chance to copy and bring a similar product into production. We attended many waste vehicle exhibitions and even got the Wastemaster fitted as original equipment to Dennis Eagle waste trucks. The Wastemaster also proved a great success on tug vehicles that work in the docks. We therefore rechristened some of the moulds with the name Tugmaster.

Our main independent competitor at the time was a company called Vaculug who operated out of Grantham. They were a bigger operation than ourselves and also retreaded earthmover tyres. They were suppliers to Tesco, but again through a tyre distributor. It seemed that there was a way to work with a large end-user and a tyre distributor. We were informed by the NTS sales person that Tesco were having problems with their present retreader and there could be an opportunity for us. He would arrange a meeting with the buyer. We set up some tyre tests against our competitors and the tyres performed well and our price worked out to be lower per kilometre than our competitors'. My brother John and the NTS sales person had a meeting

The Wastemaster gave us a leap forward

with the buyer and hammered out a deal for Bandvulc to become the replacement retread supplier. Our main sales person at this time was a young guy in his twenties called Philip West. Philip had recently left school and came to work in our warehouse. He was a very competitive person and had done a few local calls with a good deal of success. We promoted him to sales manager and he really took to the role. He quickly formed a good working relationship with the Tesco staff and the addition of such a large fleet increased our sales dramatically. We developed a detailed reporting system to feed back to Tesco, the condition of the tyres being removed from their fleet. We called it Complete Casing Control or Triple C for short. This enabled us to work closer with them to reduce their tyre costs. We could identify damaged tyres and where the damage was occurring, we could also hold back tyres that had failed prematurely because of manufacturing faults, tyres that had been poorly maintained because of low tyre pressure or axle misalignment. Then came the day at one of our annual Tesco review meetings where we asked for a price rise as we hadn't had one for two years. They said that the prices of products in their stores were cheaper than two years ago, they had achieved this by managing their costs down and we should do the same. Feeling rather deflated we sat there but then they asked the $6,000,000 question. They were disbanding their own in-house tyre team and wanted one supplier who could offer taking over all of their tyre service paperwork. Did we have the facilities to take this on for a fee? "Of course we can!" came our reply. "How much?" they asked. We had a quick chat and came up with a figure of one thousand pounds a week which we gave to them. We knew from inside information that it was costing them about five thousand pounds a week to manage it themselves. They gave the standard horrified look but we stuck out at the price and they eventually agreed. They gave us a month in order to set up the system. Our initial tyre management system consisted of two plastic trays. One for collecting the incoming job sheets and then one for holding the job sheets when they had been entered. The system worked well enough to process all of their paperwork and approve payment on work that had been carried out and tyres supplied. We could manage it with one person fulltime and so we had our price rise in a roundabout

Leading the field at Brands Hatch

Truck Racing Champion Roy Clarke

Truck Racing Team

way. There were some 'rumblings' from the service providers that we worked with, about us getting too close to who they considered were their customers but we managed to keep them all on side.

In the meantime we had started to take marketing seriously and took part in many exhibitions and events. A group of guys in Somerset who worked for a transport company approached us to see if we would sponsor them with their racing truck. Roy Clarke would be the driver. In his past, Roy had been quite a successful stock car driver. They seemed enthusiastic and would carry out all the work in their own time, if we supplied the tyres and parts that were required. They started out with a Bedford TM with a six-cylinder Detroit engine which is a diesel two stroke that emits a very unusual exhaust noise often heard on older American movies. The truck gave them some good experience but the design of it could not compete with the long bonnet American style trucks. We then bought an American Road Boss truck which had a Cummins engine. This proved much more successful until Roy, after coming down the straight at Brands Hatch at 100 miles per hour took his foot off the accelerator pedal to take the corner only to find the linkage had dropped off and he was stuck at full power. He hit the barrier at full speed and wrote the truck off, but fortunately walked away with just cuts and bruises and a dented ego. We then purchased another Road Boss from the States and this one proved to be even more successful. We went into truck racing not knowing much about trying to make a tyre that would perform under extreme conditions. We weren't even sure that we could learn anything from the project, but we learnt plenty. The main thing seemed to be to have a solid continuous outer shoulder on the tyre. Any sign of lugs or grooves would make the handing unpredictable and cause Roy to voice his criticism in a very forceful manner. The other design feature was that the tyre tread had to be as flat as possible in order that as much of the tread as could be gained would be in contact with the track. The combination of the shoulder design and the flat profile enabled the driver to control the side slip in corners and not experience a sudden break away. My brother John also formulated a special rubber compound that as the tyres got hot they appeared to 'sweat' and get sticky. Roy would often return to the pits with all sorts of paper and

Bandvulc call centre

cardboard stuck to his tyres. Truck Racing put our name out there in front of a lot of small trucking companies and although it was hard to judge, I think it brought us in more national business.

The new production facility had been designed with conveyors and lifting equipment that meant the handling and processing of the tyres became much more efficient. We started to ship tyres to Germany and developed a working relationship with a tyre distributor called Vergolst. They were owned by Continental Tyres but had shut down their own retreading factory and were now looking for a reliable alternative.

Another development then took place with Tesco. They said that they wanted to contract-out their total tyre contract and run it on a fixed price basis. "We tell you how many trucks and trailers we have and how many miles we drive in a year and you give us a fixed monthly bill." This would mean having a 24/7 call centre and supplying new tyres plus dedicated tyre service centres for each Tesco depot. We hurriedly set up an inhouse call centre and made arrangements with a new tyre manufacturer to supply the new tyres. A department was set up that employed call centre staff with a manager to run it. We then established tyre depots that were close to the operating Tesco distribution centres. The system worked well and our turnover increased dramatically as we were now buying and selling new tyres as well as our own retreads and also paying tyre distributors to supply our contracts. Other supermarkets then cottoned on to this system and we set them up as well. We didn't realise it but we had struck gold. The supermarket depots are big centres and use a lot of tyres. A successful tyre distributor could generate considerable income by us selecting them to service a depot. It gave us a lever to 'request' that in return for us giving them a supermarket depot, they would promote our products for their free trade sales. These free trade sales are for trucks that just roll up at depots and request a set of replacement tyres. So how could we hold our own against large organisations such as Michelin who have their own fitting depots? Michelin owned their own depots called ATS or Euromaster and at the time they were obliged to use these for their contracts. Some of these depots might be close to a customer's premises but some may be a long way away from them. With our system we could select a tyre depot close by. We also made up a network of 'friendly' tyre depots who carried our stock and would turn out 24/7 to attend roadside breakdowns. Ryan, our son, had obtained a degree in Computer Science and put together a call-out programme for our call centres to use. When a driver called in with a tyre problem, the telephone operator could pinpoint his location on a map and find the nearest supporting tyre depot to attend and confirm that they had tyres in stock. Another big supermarket that we supplied through an independent tyre distributor appeared on our radar. Asda had been using our tyres but was not under our control. The owner of Tyre Maintenance wished to retire and so we bought the business and depots and acquired complete control of Asda's tyre contract. By now 75 per cent of the country's groceries were being delivered on Bandvulc tyres.

We also supplied another large UK fleet called Christian Salvesen. They were expanding quickly into Europe and suggested that we might like to consider supplying tyres to a fleet they were taking over in Germany called Wohlfahrt. This sounded like a good addition to our present German operation with Vergolst. We set out to work out the fleet size, tyre depots, etc. Just when we thought the project was about to go ahead we were called to Salvesen HQ and told that they had bought a fleet in Spain called Gerposa and could we start right away or else they would have to find someone else to cover it, but they only wanted one tyre supplier and casing collector for their whole fleet. Our answer was: "Of course we can." We had taken on a student graduate called Stefanie Russel who was fluent in German and dealt with Vergolst and was very good at spreadsheets and presentations. She was my sidekick and really helpful in setting up the contracts. She was a friendly person but knew how to get tough when it required it; truck operations being male dominated. We didn't really know how to start to put together a network in a country I had never visited and where we had no contacts. The first thing to do was to go on a fact finding mission to Gerposa HQ in Santander. We set up a meeting and also a meeting with Euromaster, their tyre distributor. Now as I have said before, Euromaster is owned by Michelin who didn't particularly like us very much. The meeting was attended by Euromaster's European coordinator, a Dutchman called Eric van Geel. I have found the Dutch to be very pragmatic and Eric was no exception. As well as Dutch, Eric spoke English, French, German and a certain amount of Spanish. Salvesen had instructed Euromaster to work with us, and to be fair to Eric he played ball, probably hoping to find some way to trip us up and get Michelin back in, in the future. The pricing was agreed but how were we going to distribute the tyres and collect the casings back to one point? Suddenly we had a brainwave, Gerposa were distributors throughout Spain; could they stock and distribute our tyres from their warehouse HQ in Santander? No problem, came the reply. There was one stipulation from Euromaster, that all retreads that we supplied had to be on Michelin casings. Again, "No problem."

Everything seemed to quickly fall into place and we set the system up with monthly casing inspections on site in Santander. We could fly to Bilbao from Bristol and hire a car for an hour's drive to Santander. The system worked well and the tyres all behaved themselves, even on the sugar tankers that were operating in Andalucia in the summer at 40 degrees Celsius. I have to admit it now, that Michelin made a damn good casing.

We now had Spain and Germany up and running only to be told in 2001 that Salvesen had now acquired a fleet in France called Darfeuille. We met with Euromaster France and attempted to roll out our system that we had developed for Spain. All seemed to be going well when Euromaster now bowled us a bit of a curved ball. When they fitted a tyre they made a service charge which included a new valve, recutting the tyre and puncture repair and anything else the tyre may require maintenance wise. Salvesen flatly refused to pay for anything they weren't getting. In the UK and Spain they paid for service as it was carried out. France of course did things differently and being the home of Michelin they weren't going to make it easy. It seemed that no one would give way on this point. We came to a stalemate in the room. The system that we had adopted with Salvesen was that all the tyre invoices came via ourselves which we checked and then re-billed to Salvesen. We bought back any acceptable casings in the deal. We stopped for coffee and the only way I could see of moving things forward was for us to pay the blanket service charge and somehow

John and I

recharge each component of it as it was supplied. We had to rely on Euromaster telling us when they had fitted a valve or had recut a tyre which to be fair they mostly did.

At this time Bandvulc took foreign university students on work experience placements, many via the Leonardo da Vinci learning programme. By the time we had started working in Europe we had already had a range of students from various European countries. For the Salvesen contracts we had our own full time Stef who was fluent in German but we also had Carole from Spain and Olivia from France. We tended to find the European girls more ambitious than their male equivalents, which was surprising as they were working in a very male dominated industry. The three girls became known as O'Connell's Angels by the Salvesen staff. By mid-2001, Salvesen appeared to have successfully completed its transition to a dedicated logistics group, particularly after winning a record ten-year, £260 million contract with British supermarket giant Tesco. In 2007, an aggressive buyout bid for the cold storage and haulage parts of Salvesen was launched by another competitor, Norbert Dentressangle. Being a French company they used Michelin tyres and so we lost the business to our arch enemy. Salvesen had, however, taught us a lot about exporting and setting up supply and logistics operations in Europe and I am very grateful for the roller coaster ride that we enjoyed in servicing that contract.

In the meantime our success as a tyre management and retreading company was getting us noticed. We started producing retreads for other large tyre manufacturers under their own name, the most prominent of these being the German tyre manufacturer Continental. We invested in even more sophisticated software designed by Ryan who spent several hours designing and perfecting the system.

During the 2000s my nephew Patrick O'Connell took over as Managing Director and my brother John and I started to take a step back from the day to day running of the business. John did keep up his interest in developing new tyre tread compounds and I focused on the plant services plus still organising customer social events. We were founding members of a charity called Transaid which came into being as an offshoot of Save the Children and has HRH The Princess Royal

HRH

as its patron. Transaid is a charity primarily supported by UK logistics companies and does a lot of good work mainly in Africa. It does not give money but offers its services as a provider of transport solutions. A couple of examples are firstly the transporting of pregnant women to maternity hospitals. A system was developed to train local taxi drivers to carry out this function and in return they received a priority pass at the taxi ranks. Also transporting sick people can be done much quicker and cheaper with a motorbike and trailer than a four-wheel drive vehicle.

The Princess Royal was very supportive of Bandvulc, to such an extent that she came and opened one of our new buildings and together with Barclays Bank, allowed us to hire Buckingham Palace for an evening to entertain our customers.

The Bandvulc factory was now becoming a very slick operation with the investment in robots and my nephew Patrick and Tony Mailling, our production director, began to really streamline the production. As tyres of a certain size and pattern rolled off the end of the production line the computer system would tell the robot loader to select another suitable casing to start its journey along the production line. We had adopted a Camelot theme for all the production and management systems. This added a certain fun element to our production line. Ryan's call centre management system was called Galahad. The maintenance system was named Merlin and each of the tyre preparation bays were named after a knight of the Round Table.

In 2011 a disaster suddenly hit in the shape of a fire. We had spent a lot of time and money working with our insurers and the local fire officer to ensure that the buildings and processes were safe from fire. Fire was a well-known hazard in retreading factories. We had installed sprinkler systems, smoke detectors, fire doors, fire hoses and pretty much anything that would prevent a fire or stop it spreading in the event that one started. However we got caught out by a series of stupid coincidences that burnt one of our main production buildings down. All the extraction machinery and silos had been built outside of the tyre buffing hall. The extractors were large 40 hp motors built onto a plinth against the building and about ten feet up in the air. The pipes carrying the rubber dust from the buffing machines ran out through

The aftermath of the Bandvulc fire August 2011

the walls and into the extractors. The extractors then shot the dust up into silos which were emptied into half tonne sacks from the bottom of the tower. We had a Bandvulc Tyres sign that had been removed and replaced by a larger one. The sign was made of plastic and measured about three feet by one foot. As it had been lying around for a while we put it on the side of the building above the extraction tower. An unforeseen series of events now took place. A lump of hot rubber had shot out of the exhaust at the top of one of the silo towers and landed back on the platform where the extractor motors were located. There was some fine rubber dust lying on the platform where it landed and it continued to smoulder among this dust and eventually started a small fire on the platform. The fire was directly under the plastic Bandvulc sign that we had put up and this caught fire and fell onto the platform causing a bigger fire. The flames from this fire went up the side of the building and reached a point where the steel cladding overlapped the brickwork. The flames then went up the inside of the cladding and inside the building. They went up into the roof cladding which caught fire. The sprinklers now kicked in, but of course the fire was above them. I was at home at the time and got a call from Ryan telling me that there was a fire. Fortunately he had been quick thinking and shut down all the electric supply to the building. The fire brigade arrived but refused to enter the building as they said they would not enter a burning building if no one's life was at risk. We said that the fire was only in the roof area and they could easily extinguish it but they were resolute and so we had to sit and watch the building gradually burn down. The building was completely gutted but fortunately the sprinkler system had saved the buffing machines although they were now completely waterlogged. My brother John and I had managed to sneak around the back of the building during the fire and trip the fire door that isolated the fire building to the rest of the factory. We emerged black and wet from the building only to see all our staff silently stood out in the road. Production had come to a halt and we needed to get going somehow asap. When you are supplying blue chip companies they do not wish to hear tales of woe and non-supply, they will just go straight to one of your competitors. We had a fall back situation for the call centre whereby the operators could work from home and so this was immediately implemented. We notified our insurers who were very good and sent an expert to assess the situation. The insurers were also keen to get us up and running asap as we had a loss of production cover with them.

It was going to take a lot of work to get some sort of production going anytime soon especially as the event happened on a Friday afternoon and suppliers would be closed over the weekend.

We arrived back on site early on Saturday morning. The insurers arrived with the dehumidifiers and built a sort of tent around each buffing machine and ran them full belt day and night. The site of the fire was now filthy and covered with charred tyre remains. A lot of people suddenly appeared at the site. At first we thought they were just sightseers turned up for a look, but no, they were our staff, local people and previous employees who were all keen to help in any way they could. They all set about clearing and washing the floor areas and tipping the debris into some newly rented skips. We managed to rebuild the extraction system with spare parts that we carried and got it operating by Saturday evening. All the debris was cleared from around the buffing area which was a separate bay within the building. This small area of the building was the only part that was sprinklered and so was mainly wet charred rubber. We all worked throughout the weekend and by Monday we were running again at 80 per cent capacity. The temporary system required a lot of manhandling and storing of tyres at different sites but we managed to keep the production moving. It seems an odd thing to say, but the fire renewed a challenge in us all to attack and beat a new problem, which we did with gusto. The insurance assessors of course came up with a huge cost to rebuild the facility and said that we were 20 per cent under insured. We said OK, give us the insurance money and we will arrange the rebuilding ourselves, which is what we did.

We rebuilt the buffing hall with a new more efficient layout and made the building a much lighter and cleaner environment in which to work.

Richard O'Connell

Part of the Bandvulc Empire

Chapter 10

And in Conclusion

By the year 2015 Bandvulc was running better than it ever had, producing circa 4,500 truck tyres per week and supplying and fitting a large amount of new tyres. We had acquired tyre fitting depots and also expanded our warehousing. Continental Tyres then made an offer to buy us out. This caused a lot of sleepless nights. On the one side we had a very successful company employing around 450 people but on the other there were threats starting to appear. The Chinese were selling tyres in Europe, cheaper than we could make a retread. In fact, they were selling tyres cheaper than we could buy the raw material. Our government and Brussels didn't seem to think this was a problem. They could not appreciate the benefit to the environment that retreads give. Every tyre that we retreaded saved on average 44 kilograms of rubber compound and 68 litres of oil compared to making a new tyre and then dumping it. Our production alone was saving the planet 198,000 kilograms of rubber and 306,000 litres of oil. Just to add insult to injury we also had to pay 100 per cent of the climate change levy, which is a pollution tax applied to manufacturing companies. If we had made new tyres we could have claimed an exemption to the tax based on the fact that being a high energy user it would affect our profitability. The argument that recycling requires a much higher labour input compared to manufacturing a new product also had no impact on the powers that be.

We entered into negotiations with Continental and in the strict proviso that the production would remain in the UK for at least the next ten years. There then came the usual several months of horse trading but eventually a deal was struck in July 2016. Our lawyers were based in Bristol and we had to travel there on the eve of the takeover to sign the company over to Continental. What should have been a straight forward transaction turned into a very long night. One of the documents from Continental's side had not been signed and the person concerned could not be located. A search was set out to find him and at about 3 am he was traced and signed the outstanding document. We left Bristol and arrived home at about 5 am and were ready for bed.

Next day the UK MD of Continental arrived at the factory along with his accountant and we planned the announcement to the staff which was to be made the following morning.

When the following morning came we gathered everyone in the factory and made the announcement that Continental would be taking over the business from henceforth. I think there was some slight relief from everyone that we weren't closing down and their jobs were safe. John and I left the premises immediately after the meeting but John's son Patrick and my son Ryan stayed on for a period of time. Ryan's wife Romy, who is German, and came to us on a work experience programme stayed on with the company in the accounts department and remains there to this day.

Passing on the ownership somehow felt a betrayal. Over the years we had overcome all sorts of obstacles and with each, we had gathered strength and moved forward. Now we, the family, who had created this pulsating hive of activity were turning our backs on it and walking away.

It made me recall, though, what our Dad had said to John and me when he was getting too old to run the farm. "I bought the farm because it was something I always wanted to do, if you want to continue with it, take it on, if not Mum and I will sell it and retire and you can follow your own ambitions." I felt John and I were now in the same position. We had taken truck tyre retreading, from having a dubious cheap tyre replacement image, to being a high quality replacement tyre and used and specified by many blue chip distribution companies. Those early days in 1971 when we could barely make five tyres per day, to 2016 when a Bandvulc tyre was being fitted every three minutes 24/7.

I am still not really retired. We have invested in commercial and domestic properties plus I am involved in local community groups, local politics and am also a STEM (Science, Technology, Engineering, Maths) for schools, trying to get our young people interested in following a similar path to myself. It has been one heck of a journey but retreading it has been fun.

John and I taking our final walk through the factory

www.ingramcontent.com/pod-product-compliance
Lightning Source LLC
Chambersburg PA
CBHW071213070526
44584CB00019B/3021